HORACE | THE ODES

FACING PAGES

FACING PAGES

NICHOLAS JENKINS

Series Editor

EDITED BY J. D. McCLATCHY

New translations by

Robert Bly
Eavan Boland
Robert Creeley
Dick Davis
Mark Doty
Alice Fulton
Debora Greger
Linda Gregerson
Rachel Hadas
Donald Hall
Robert Hass
Anthony Hecht
Daryl Hine
John Hollander
Richard Howard
John Kinsella
Carolyn Kizer

James Lasdun
J. D. McClatchy
Heather McHugh
W. S. Merwin
Paul Muldoon
Carl Phillips
Robert Pinsky
Marie Ponsot
Charles Simic
Mark Strand
Charles Tomlinson
Ellen Bryant Voigt
David Wagoner
Rosanna Warren
Richard Wilbur
C. K. Williams
Charles Wright
Stephen Yenser

HORACE | THE ODES

New Translations by Contemporary Poets

PRINCETON UNIVERSITY PRESS

Princeton and Oxford

Copyright © 2002 by Princeton University Press

Published by Princeton University Press, 41 William Street, Princeton,
New Jersey 08540

In the United Kingdom: Princeton University Press, 3 Market Place,
Woodstock, Oxfordshire OX20 1SY

Library of Congress Cataloging-in-Publication Data
Horace.

    Horace, the Odes / new translations by contemporary poets, Robert Bly ... [et al.] ;
edited by J. D. McClatchy.

      p. cm. — (Facing pages)

    Includes index.

    ISBN 0-691-04919-X (cloth : alk. paper)

    1. Horace—Translations into English.   2. Laudatory poetry, Latin—Translations
into English. I. Bly, Robert. II. McClatchy, J. D., 1945– III. Title. IV. Series.
PA6394 .A2 2002

874′.01—dc21   2002023128

British Library Cataloging-in-Publication Data is available

This book is supported by the Charles Lacy Lockert Fund of Princeton University Press.

This book has been composed in Akzidenz-Grotesk and Minion

Printed on acid-free paper. ∞

www.pupress.princeton.edu

Printed in the United States of America

10 9 8 7 6 5 4 3 2

CONTENTS

INTRODUCTION

Between them, schoolboys and poets define the range of attitudes towards the odes of Horace, and in a sense embody the change that may occur in most any reader towards this group of poems that have, since they were first published, been considered the epitome of lyric poetry. One's first brush with them can be memorable, but for all the wrong reasons. It was Byron who wrote, "Then farewell, Horace—whom I hated so." The classroom ruins Horace. No one has better described the dry horror than Rudyard Kipling in his story "Regulus," published in 1908, where timorous boys are drilled and humiliated by the martinet memory makes out of any demanding teacher. Mr. King, the Latin master, has young Beetle in his pincers. Beetle is standing before the class, translating Horace's great ode, the fifth poem of the third book, that tells the story of the Roman general Regulus, whose sense of duty leads to his death. A thrilling fable and a vivid poem are all reduced to sawdust in the mouth.

> '*Credidimus*, we—believe—we have believed,' he opened in hesitating slow time, '*tonantem Jovem*, thundering Jove—*regnare*, to reign—*caelo*, in heaven. *Augustus*, Augustus—*habebitur*, will be held or considered—*praesens divus*, a present God—*adjectis Britannis*, the Britons being added—*imperio*, to the Empire—*gravibusque Persis*, with the heavy—er, stern Persians.'
>
> 'What?'
>
> 'The grave or stern Persians.' Beetle pulled up with the 'Thank-God-I-have-done-my-duty' air of Nelson in the cockpit.
>
> 'I am quite aware,' said King, 'that the first stanza is about the extent of your knowledge, but continue, sweet one, continue. *Gravibus*, by the way, is usually translated as "troublesome."'

1

I can remember that sort of scene in my own education. To the young eye, Horace is a chore, and his poems must seem like those noble statues in the corridors of the Vatican Museum, for centuries considered paragons but today often scurried by.

Lucky readers, however, return to Horace later in life and find what they could not earlier see—a whole world elegantly suspended in poems that brim with a wisdom alternately sly and sad. In this, the fortunate ones resemble the poets. Down the centuries, writers have been exhilarated by Horace's example, and turned to his poems as an inspiration for their own. It takes a certain need, a certain knowingness that comes with age. There is another classroom scene, quite different from Kipling's, that makes the point. It was May of 1914, and Cambridge undergraduates were crowded in to hear A. E. Housman lecture on Horace. The trees outside were heavy with blossoms, and no doubt most of the students—so many of them soon to die in the Great War—could recite Housman's own poem, "Loveliest of trees, the cherry now / Is hung with bloom along the bough. . . ." Tenderest of poets, Housman was an intimidating, sarcastic teacher. The subject of his lecture that day was the seventh ode of the fourth book, one of Horace's most famous and melancholy: *Diffugere nives, redeunt iam gramina campis.* Housman took it apart and put it back together in a brilliant display of scholarship. Then, the account continues, he looked up at the class—the first time he had deigned to notice them in two years—and in an eerily quiet voice said, "I should like to spend the last few minutes considering this ode simply as poetry." With deep emotion, he read the poem aloud, first in Latin, and then in his own peerless English translation.

> The snows are fled away, leaves on the shaws
>   And grasses in the mead renew their birth,
> The river to the river-bed withdraws,
>   And altered is the fashion of the earth.
>
> The Nymphs and Graces three put off their fear
>   And unapparelled in the woodland play.
> The swift hour and the brief prime of the year
>   Say to the soul, *Thou wast not born for aye.*
>
> Thaw follows frost; hard on the heel of spring
>   Treads summer sure to die, for hard on hers
> Comes autumn, with his apples scattering;
>   Then back to wintertide, when nothing stirs.

But oh, whate'er the sky-led seasons mar,
 Moon upon moon rebuilds it with her beams:
Come *we* where Tullus and where Ancus are,
 And good Aeneas, we are dust and dreams.

Torquatus, if the gods in heaven shall add
 The morrow to the day, what tongue has told?
Feast then thy heart, for what thy heart has had
 The fingers of no heir will ever hold.

When thou descendest once the shades among,
 The stern assize and equal judgment o'er,
Not thy long lineage nor thy golden tongue,
 No, nor thy righteousness, shall friend thee more.

Night holds Hippolytus the pure of stain,
 Diana steads him nothing, he must stay;
And Theseus leaves Pirithöus in the chain
 The love of comrades cannot take away.

The students grew uncomfortable, and thought they saw tears in the old man's eyes. "That," they remembered him saying in the tone of a man betraying a secret, "I regard as the most beautiful poem in ancient literature." He turned abruptly and hurried out of the room.

Poets before and since have been as similarly moved by Horace's gravity as they have been enchanted by his insouciance. John Milton once translated the famous fifth ode of the first book, one of literature's most beguiling and wry love poems. It is addressed to a former mistress named Pyrrha, and Milton—proud to have rendered it "according to the Latin measure, as near as the language will permit"—begins it this way:

What slender youth, bedewed with liquid odours,
Courts thee on roses in some pleasant cave,
 Pyrrha? For whom bind'st thou
 In wreaths thy golden hair . . .

The poet seems to have had this passage in mind when, in the fourth book of *Paradise Lost,* he describes Adam and Eve in Eden:

These, lulled by nightingales, embracing slept,
And on their naked limbs the flowery roof
Showered roses.

The mention of nightingales reminds one of Keats sitting under a tree, a volume of Horace open on his knee, reading the start of the fourteenth epode:

Why a soft numbness drenches all my inmost senses with deep oblivion,
As though with thirsty throat I'd drained the cup that brings a sleep as
    low as Lethe . . .

And then he started his "Ode to a Nightingale":

My heart aches, and a drowsy numbness pains
    My sense, as though of hemlock I had drunk,
Or emptied some dull opiate to the drains
    One minute past, and Lethe-wards had sunk . . .

It is not merely the ravishing lines that attract the poets. It is the temperament: not so much Horace as the Horatian. W. H. Auden saw a flock of Horatians scattered through history, people who fled crowds, traffic noises, bluestockings, and millionaires, to content themselves in obscure positions, desiring only a genteel sufficiency, content to impress only their friends and their dogs. Auden goes on about the type, and then addresses the old poet himself:

                    Enthusiastic
Youth writes you off as cold, who cannot be found on
        barricades, and never shoot
        either yourselves or your lovers.

You thought well of your Odes, Flaccus, and believed they
would live, but knew, and have taught your descendants to
        say with you: "As makers go,
        compared with Pindar or any

of the great foudroyant masters who don't ever
amend, we are, for all our polish, of little
        stature, and, as human lives,
        compared with authentic martyrs

4

like Regulus, of no account. We can only
do what it seems to us we were made for, look at
    this world with a happy eye
    but from a sober perspective."

In a way, Auden's Horatian strain is a note many poets—once they've put aside their singing robes, once they think of themselves as craftsmen rather than as bards, once they attend the world as a surgery and not a party—long to strike, and in their maturity often do. Wisdom and its hard lessons have become their goal: what cannot be had, what must be let go, the whole economy of desire and power.

From Ben Jonson to Robert Lowell, from Sir Philip Sidney and Robert Herrick to William Wordsworth, Gerard Manley Hopkins, and Basil Bunting, our leading poets have been drawn to bring over individual odes into English. (There have been notable amateurs as well, like John Quincy Adams and William Ewart Gladstone.) Some, like Alexander Pope, are naturals; his imitations of the epistles are one of English poetry's chief glories. Dryden too catches Horace's tone so exactly and carries it so felicitously into English that this part of his paraphrase of III.29 seems to belong to our language:

    Happy the man, and happy he alone,
        He, who can call to day his own:
        He, secure within, can say
    To morrow do thy worst, for I have liv'd to day.
        Be fair, or foul, or rain, or shine,
    The joys I have possest, in spight of fate are mine.
        Not Heav'n it self upon the past has pow'r;
    But what has been, has been, and I have had my hour.

Never before, though, have the leading poets of the day assembled specifically to translate all the odes. The versions here have been specially commissioned for this book, and together are a unique occasion. There have been brave individuals intent on doing the whole job themselves, but this collaborative effort brings different imaginative energies to bear on a joint project and is a rare treasure. Horace, in fact, thought of himself as a translator, and considered his true distinction to have been a "gift for turning Greek verse into Latin," an ability to adapt old ways to new times. It was in that spirit that the poets in this book worked. The results, inevitably, vary in ways the work of a single hand would not. Some poets worked close to the Latin bone, sometimes in the original meters. Others wrote more freely: Horace's stanzas are reshaped, rhymes are added or free verse deployed, the looser rhythms of English verse dominate. This is as it should be. *Horace, The Odes* is not offered as a crib, but as a series of collaborations, a meeting of minds. Any translation will depart from the precisions of the original; the point is to head not down the rutted prosaic road but along fresh routes. This book draws on three dozen remarkable sensibilities, each in command of a formidable technique, yet able to submit that talent to Horace's own preoccupations, his brooding sense of belatedness and guilt as he surveys the course of empire and the claims of mortality. In fact, the variety of tone to be heard in these translations matches the mercurial shifts in mood and response the Latin poems themselves exhibit. The pairings of poem and translator were deliberate, and made in the hope of creating interesting juxtapositions. To have an American poet laureate write about political patronage, to have a woman poet write about seduction, an old poet write about the vagaries of age, a Southern poet about the blandishments of the countryside, a gay poet about the strategies of "degeneracy" . . . these are part of the editorial plot for this new book.

A few poets, pleading their fuzzy memories of old Latin classes, begged off, and even those who accepted my invitation did so with a certain hesitation. After all, the poetic challenge is daunting. Nietzsche once referred to Horace's work as a "mosaic of words in which every word diffuses its force by sound, position and idea, right and left, over the whole." But then, each had been asked because of his or her mastery of English rather than of Latin in the enterprise "to make the Eccho equall with the voice," and there was no one who did not in the end remark to me on the literally thrilling time spent with Horace's lines, with his world, with his voice, with his incomparable command of the moral and emotional stakes. The book you hold now in your hand is the result of, again and again, one poet confronting another, each of our contemporaries alone with the man who first gave us the lyrics by which we have understood the nature and duty of poetry itself.

Quintus Horatius Flaccus was born on December 8, 65 B.C. in the town of Venusia, in the remote province of Apulia, near the heel of Italy. It was an arid, rocky, impoverished area, and the boy's prospects were dim. His father had been a slave, whether a kidnapped foreigner or a prisoner of war we don't know. By the time Horace was born, however, his father had been freed. Though the poet never mentions his mother, several times in his work he writes of his admiration for his father. How a freedman accumulated enough money to educate his son remains a mystery. Horace himself tells us his father was "poor on a meager farm"; there is other evidence that he may have worked as an auctioneer's agent or dealer in merchandise. In any case, whether he sold the farm or was a resourceful entrepreneur, he was determined to give his young son the best possible education. He took his money and moved the boy to Rome, where he was sent to the finest schools. Horace never forgot his stern tutor Orbilius, who applied the cane and drilled the boy in Homer. But neither did he ever forget his father, who, if he spoiled the boy, still sought for his son a strong moral discipline. As Horace later wrote in one of his *Satires*:

> My clothes, and the servants following me,
> would seem to anyone, passing in the crowd, so rich,
> they must have come from an old and proud inheritance.
> And he himself, most incorruptible of guardians,
> escorted me to all my teachers. Thus he kept me
> pure—the first reward of virtue—not only in deed,
> but pure even from the slightest shadow of disgrace.

To finish his education, Horace was next sent to Athens. He studied philosophy, Plato as well as the Stoic and Epicurean teachings. More crucially, he studied the old literature—Pindar, Sappho, Alcaeus, Anacreon—and even wrote poems in Greek himself, acquiring thereby a mastery of the intricate meters and tonal nuances that distinguished Greek literature from its plainer Roman copies. Greek literature, it might be said, became his homeland: a familiar, beloved landscape. From the Greeks he learned that power resides in discipline; that a sophisticated technique alone possesses the subtle buoyancy to rise above the ordinary; and that wisdom, rather than finesse or sincerity or bluster, is finally the true source of poetic strength.

While in Greece, though, he was caught up, as young men are, in the political events of the day. Julius Caesar had been assassinated, and Horace was drawn to the struggling republican cause. He enlisted as a military tribune in the doomed army of the exiled Marcus Brutus, fought at Philippi, and later wrote of himself as if he were a character in Homer: that, trembling in the great battle, he dropped his shield and had to be rescued by Mercury, who wrapped him in a mist to save his life. His father having died in the meanwhile, he returned to Rome in disgrace, his property confiscated. But by 41 B.C., following Octavian's general amnesty, Horace had secured for himself a position as a scribe in the civil service.

It was during this period that he published his first poems, his *Epodes* and early *Satires*. Their suave sarcasms drew the attention of readers and of other poets, most notably the young Virgil, who befriended Horace and, in 39 B.C., helped introduce him to Rome's rich taste-maker and patron, the estimable

Maecenas. Some months passed before an overture came, but Maecenas, impressed by the poet's promise, soon granted him an income sufficient to quit his post and move to the outskirts of Rome. The town of Tibur—present-day Tivoli—became a green retreat from which he ventured to the capital to observe the rush of its tumults, intrigues, and follies, and to which he returned to brood over human foibles. In addition to providing him with the leisure to write, Tibur was a moral perspective, the golden scale in which the values of urban glamour and rustic peace-of-mind could be weighed. "In Rome," he wrote, "my fancy blows me to Tibur, and in Tibur to Rome." It was here that he worked on his *Odes*. It was here that—in contrast to Pindar's example, say, the sky-storming swan—he worked like a bee, as he says in IV.2 (here in Philip Francis's 1746 translation):

> Thus when the Theban Swan attempts the Skies,
> A nobler Gale of Rapture bids Him rise;
> But like a Bee, which through the breezy Groves,
> With feeble Wing and idle Murmurs roves,
>   Sits on the Bloom, and with unceasing Toil
> From Thyme sweet-breathing culls his flowery Spoil;
> So I, weak Bard! round Tibur's lucid Spring,
> Of humble Strain laborious Verses sing.

Even Tibur made its demands, and Maecenas, sensing that the poet's delicate health and need for privacy were threatened, deeded to Horace, then thirty-two years old, a farm eight miles further away from Rome, in the Sabine hills. This is a property that Horace, in turn, made immortal, most notably in the verse epistles he wrote to friends some years later. It was a working farm, with a foreman and eight slave-laborers (whom Horace himself worked beside), with livestock, as well as orchards and fields he rented to tenants, and it produced a modest income that allowed him to live comfortably. That Horace's father once owned a farm is a tender irony. That a man who had once fought against Octavian had now come to admire him, even volunteer to return to the army to fight the rebellion of Antony that culminated at Actium, only shows how the emperor and his advisor Maecenas had won over the most intelligent of citizens. It seems to have been during this period that the emperor wrote a letter to Maecenas, one sentence of which was retrieved and quoted by Suetonius. Augustus asked his friend to persuade Horace to serve as his private secretary: "Up to the present I have been able to conduct my own private correspondence; but now I am exceedingly busy and am none too well and I should like to deprive you of our friend Horace. Accordingly, he will come away from your table where he accepts your favors gratis to my palatial board and aid me in my correspondence." Refusal must have been difficult, but Horace, perhaps mindful of his father's enslavement, did refuse the emperor's order into service, itself a form of noble slavery, with its blandishments and privileges. He may well be referring to his refusal in III.16, a poem addressed to Maecenas: *iure perhorrui / late conspicuum tollere verticem* ("with reason I shrank from raising my head to be seen afar"). Instead, for seven years, from his thirty-fifth to his forty-second year, Horace continued working on his odes.

That a poet who began as a cynical satirist should next turn to the creation of exquisite lyrics may just signal a poetic gift coming at last to its true maturity. Horace had labored for a considerable time—and a time of momentous public events—over his odes, which, when read together, display a remarkable variety and finish. Under the guise of different addresses—the occasional, the political, the didactic, the erotic, the elegiac—he wove a single lyric tapestry on which plays the light and shade of human experience. He indulges private reveries and historical meditations; his friends are praised, his enemies derided; his loves, both women and men, are teased or scorned, longed for or lost. And every song proclaims his Roman Alexandrianism, his preference for an urbane, lapidary ingenuity. When at last, in 23 B.C., he gathered eighty-eight poems together, divided among three books, and published the scrolls of his masterwork, he chose as the last poem in the series a tribute to his own powers and to their achievement:

> *Exegi monumentum aere perennius*
> *regalique situ pyramidum altius,*
> *quod non imber edax, non Aquilo impotens*
> *possit diruere aut innumerabilis*
> *annorum series et fuga temporum.*
> *non omnis moriar multaque pars mei*
> *vitabit Libitinam: usque ego postera*
> *crescam laude recens.*

This monument will outlast metal and I made it
More durable than the king's seat, higher than pyramids.
Gnaw of wind and rain?
             Impotent
The flow of years to break it, however many.

Bits of me, many bits, will dodge all funeral,
O Libitina-Persephone and, after that,
Sprout new praise.

(trans. Ezra Pound)

It seems, though, that this most important and influential book of lyric poems ever published was not especially well received by the Roman public. In any case, Horace himself was disappointed with their reception, as he says in one of his epistles:

Now shall I tell you why the ungrateful reader praises
my work and loves it at home, but disparages it in public?
I do not whistle up the winds of popularity
by giving lavish parties, handing out trashy gifts.
I cannot hear and criticize distinguished authors
on lecture-platforms and in meetings of professors.
"Hence these tears!"

(trans. Gilbert Highet)

But more discriminating readers—including the emperor himself—realized that they had been offered an incomparable gift, a work that had literally transformed Latin poetry. Augustus asked that Horace compose yet another book of odes, and ten years later, in 13 B.C., the poet published the fourth book—which opens, as if gently to mock his own enterprise, with the protest of an old lover against the renewed assaults of passion and romance. The entire book is tinged with resignation and the shivers of mortality.

Earlier, Augustus had also commissioned Horace to compose the *Carmen Saeculare,* the so-called Centennial Hymn, to be sung on June 3, 17 B.C. by a chorus of virgins and boys on the Palatine at the great public celebration of secular games meant to commemorate the span of Roman power and of its apogee under the emperor. It is the only one of Horace's poems written for public performance, and in his fourth book of odes Horace—always a contemplative, private, even retiring poet—refers to himself in newly civic terms as "a performer on Rome's lyre." Though this poem is usually placed beyond the traditional canon of his odes, it shares with them not only a technical virtuosity but a concern for the passage of time. Addressed to Apollo and Diana, the protectors of Roman grandeur, the poem looks back to the city's heroic past and heaven-sent responsibilities as a legacy to be guarded by its citizens and guided by its emperor. Governance, whether in one's private life or in the public sphere, is often the focus of Horace's lyrics, and when Pope remarked of Horace that he "*judg'd with Coolness* tho' he sung with *Fire*," he is pointing to a tension that can create a poem or should rule the state.

Towards the end of his life, he turned to finishing the twenty-three *Epistles* addressed to various of his friends. Taken together, these poems contemplate the golden mean with the graceful wit of a sensible hedonist, a superstitious *raisonneur*. As verse letters, their tone is intimate, dominated by his personality's genial astuteness rather than by the strictures of any philosophy. In these poems above all, as Pope said, "*Horace* still charms with graceful Negligence, / And without Method *talks* us into Sense." He lived out his days on his farm and died, at the age of fifty-six, on November 27, 8 B.C. At the end of his first book of *Epistles*, he had addressed his own work. "Go, little book," he wrote—

> say I was born in poverty of a father once a slave,
> but stretched my wings far beyond that humble nest:
> what you subtract from my descent, add to my virtues;
> say that I pleased the greatest Romans, in war and peace;
> say I was small, and early grey, and loved hot sunshine,
> swift to anger and yet easy to pacify . . .

(trans. Gilbert Highet)

His patron and friend Maecenas had died two months earlier, and on his deathbed had written to the emperor commending Horace and begging Augustus to "think always of him as you do of me." Suetonius tells us that Horace's last thoughts were of his two most faithful readers: on his deathbed, too weak to sign his will, he asked that his estate be given to Augustus, and that his body be buried near that of Maecenas.

The very word *ode* conjures the stiff, exclamatory celebrations of Pindar. Actually the word Horace himself used to describe these poems was *carminae* or "songs," but to call them "odes," as literary history has, conveniently emphasizes their ironic relationship to an older tradition. Where Pindar praised the victorious athlete, Horace clucks over the hapless suitor or retiring rustic; instead of hymns to honor a glistening prowess, Horace will suggest another cup of wine in the shade. It's not that he took his duties lightly. He can boast of his vatic role, as he does in III.1: *carmina non prius / audita Musarum sacerdos / virginibus puerisque canto* ("Priest of the Muses, I sing for young men and maids a song not heard before"). And in the first six odes of Book Three, the so-called "Roman Odes," Horace addresses himself rigorously to the history and ambition of Rome, or the Augustan vision of it, while recalling its bloody struggles and stern sense of duty. In poems that would have pleased his own strict father, and that undoubtedly gratified his paternal emperor, the poet wags a disapproving finger at the decline of old-fashioned standards—the very sort of straightforward moralizing that the rest of his poems, if not mock, then blithely ignore.

Any English translation of these poems, sadly, will smooth their textures and thereby flatten their effect. What the translations lack is the extraordinary versatility of Horace's line. This derives in part from his uncanny sense of rhythm and from his dramatic perspectives. How easily he moves from distant setting to intimate feelings, from literal event to figurative implication, from public discourse to private allusion, from scene to mood—as in the famous I.9, which shifts from a cold mountain vista to sweet whispered nothings, from frozen streams to a mere finger. Or watch how, in I.37, the celebrated ode about the downfall of Cleopatra, he edges away from gloating over the mad queen's death to an admiring account of her suicide, which itself allows her a triumph over her Roman enemies. Horace's own sympathies? As usual, they sidle between the extremes, darting, dreaming, delving.

Horace's poetic line also has the advantage of Latin. Unlike its inflexible English equivalent, the Latin line has the syntactical sinuosity granted by a language driven by inflection rather than placement. English words gather their meanings by their position within a sentence; Latin words, construed by their endings, can be put wherever a poet deems them most interesting. The architecture of lines is everywhere apparent in Horace's poems. Their word order is compressed and febrile. Let one example stand in for countless others. At the end of one of his most memorable and affecting poems, the first ode of his last book, his plea to Venus for an end of passion, he is dreaming of the young Ligurinus, fleeing the poet's embraces. In the dream, the boy is running across the great arena, the Campus Martius, and then, suddenly, is engulfed by the sea. It is, first of all, a convincing dream, with all the eeriness and symbolic dissolves we might expect to discover in a desperate lover's unconscious. But on top of that, Horace can place his words in an infinitely expressive manner. The final stanza in its original goes:

> *nocturnis ego somniis*
>   *iam captum teneo, iam volucrem sequor*
> *te per gramina Martii*
>   *Campi, te per aquas, dure, volubilis.*

12

"In dreams, now I hold you fast, now run after you over the field of the Campus Martius, oh hard-of-heart, and through the roiling waves." One look at the stanza and you can see the careful repetitions and contrasts. The *ego* in pursuit of *te*, and again *te*. No sooner (*iam*) had than again (*iam*) lost. And in the last line, the phrase *per aquas, dure, volubilis* puts the hardened youth between the watery terms *aquas* and *volubilis*, which can mean revolving or changeable or fluent. What is fluent, of course, is the poet's own speech, useless against the hard silence of vanishing desire—and embedded in it.

These kinds of antitheses and subtle correspondences are entirely characteristic of Horace's style, as he moves among his small paradoxes. The tone of these odes glides from the stricken to the sentimental to the skeptical, giving the poems their melodramatic edge and psychological interest. At the same time, the poet's voice is detached, cooly apart. It is the detachment of the lyric voice itself, able to contain emotion but formally exacting about its consequences. We can hear this most obviously in those magical phrases that have become commonplaces, what Tennyson once called

> jewels five-words-long
> That on the stretched forefinger of all Time
> Sparkle for ever.

And it is there we look for the *balance* that Horace's double-seeing is constantly in search of. But underneath the apparent acceptance of nature's course, stripped of false desires and fond illusions, is something else—what Goethe called "*eine furchtbar Realität*," a dark realism. It is death that haunts all of these poems. It is death—as this son of a slave would know—that levels all men and eliminates privilege, reducing each to "dust and dreams." It is death that is the spur to small pleasures. It is death that is the doorway into and out of heartache.

For all the ritual pieties of his day, Horace lived in a secular society, and when he invokes the empty formulas of divinity he is speaking of forces within us— love or power, violence or compassion, resignation or defiance. Gods and nymphs come and go in our minds as impulses or fancies. Few poets have been able to hold them for a moment, to watch and appreciate them, to render them with such an estranging elegance, to reason with us about unreason. His is the wisdom of years, the chilling consolation, the brilliance that reveals and reminds. Cloaked now in English, he walks out among us. Let him pluck your sleeve and tell his story. When you next look up, everything will have changed.

LIBER | BOOK I

Maecenas atavis edite regibus,
o et praesidium et dulce decus meum,
sunt quos curriculo pulverem Olympicum
collegisse iuvat metaque fervidis
evitata rotis palmaque nobilis
terrarum dominos evehit ad deos;
hunc, si mobilium turba Quiritium
certat tergeminis tollere honoribus;
illum, si proprio condidit horreo,
quicquid de Libycis verritur areis.
gaudentem patrios findere sarculo
agros Attalicis condicionibus
numquam demoveas, ut trabe Cypria
Myrtoum pavidus nauta secet mare.
luctantem Icariis fluctibus Africum
mercator metuens otium et oppidi
laudat rura sui; mox reficit rates
quassas, indocilis pauperiem pati.
est qui nec veteris pocula Massici
nec partem solido demere de die
spernit, nunc viridi membra sub arbuto
stratus, nunc ad aquae lene caput sacrae.
multos castra iuvant et lituo tubae
permixtus sonitus bellaque matribus
detestata. manet sub Iove frigido
venator tenerae coniugis immemor,
seu visa est catulis cerva fidelibus,
seu rupit teretes Marsus aper plagas.
me doctarum hederae praemia frontium
dis miscent superis, me gelidum nemus
nympharumque leves cum Satyris chori
secernunt populo, si neque tibias
Euterpe cohibet nec Polyhymnia
Lesboum refugit tendere barbiton.
quodsi me lyricis vatibus inseris,
sublimi feriam sidera vertice.

I. 1

Maecenas, my protector, descendant of kings,
Friend, fountain of honor—in this world different things
Give different people joy. Some feel it most
In racing: wheels flashing through the Olympic dust,
Their chariot speeds around the turn to come
Thundering to the finish first, and win the palm—
Mastery on earth that makes them feel like gods.
Some crave the vote of the fickle Roman crowds;
And some, the knowledge that Libya's threshing floors
Have been swept clean to fill their private stores.
The peasant loves to scratch his bit of dirt,
And no amount of money could convert
Him to a sailor, trembling as he ploughs
Across the ocean. And though the ocean cows
The merchant who starts to weep for his valley home
During a ferocious storm, as soon as it's calm
He's busy fitting his boats for some new journey,
Not having learned the knack of going hungry.
Many love wine, and always steal some time
From the busy day to drink by a shady stream.
Many men crave the excitement of a war,
Thrilled by the call to battle that mothers abhor.
Under the cold stars, far from his wife's warm bed,
The passionate hunter is happy to be led
By his hounds' voices to discover a deer
Or a wild pig that's broken through the snare.

It's a wreath of ivy, crown of poets, that I
Need, to believe I'm among the gods on high.
It's the lyric dance of satyrs and nymphs I love—
Woven by the muses in a secret grove
Hidden from the crowd, where Euterpe tunes the flute
And Polyhymnia keeps the lyre-strings sweet:
Count me among the poets, and I feel like a god—
Bumping the stars with my exalted head.

Robert Pinsky

I. 2

Iam satis terris nivis atque dirae
grandinis misit Pater et rubente
dextera sacras iaculatus arces
    terruit urbem,

terruit gentis, grave ne rediret
saeculum Pyrrhae nova monstra questae,
omne cum Proteus pecus egit altos
    visera montes,

piscium et summa genus haesit ulmo,
nota quae sedes fuerat columbis,
et superiecto pavidae natarunt
    aequore dammae.

vidimus flavum Tiberim, retortis
litore Etrusco violenter undis,
ire deiectum monumenta regis
    templaque Vestae,

Iliae dum se nimium querenti
iactat ultorem, vagus et sinistra
labitur ripa, Iove non probante, ux-
    orius amnis.

audiet civis acuisse ferrum,
quo graves Persae melius perirent,
audiet pugnas vitio parentum
    rara iuventus.

quem vocet divom populus ruentis
imperi rebus? Prece qua fatigent
virgines sanctae minus audientem
    carmina Vestam?

I.2

It's enough now, all this vicious snow and hail
Father Jupiter has sent to earth, enough
his striking sacred peaks with a smoldering hand
    to terrify the town,

to terrify the people: what if the dismal age
of Pyrrha should return, when she quailed at strange
new signs, when Proteus drove his ocean herd
    to visit mountaintops,

and the race of fish clustered in the highest elms
where doves used to build their nests in the dry old days,
and deer swam, terrified, in floods ravening
    over the lost land?

We saw the mustard Tiber, his waves flung back
passionately from the Tuscan shore, roar up
to batter King Numa's monuments, and swamp
    the vestal shrines—

the river god too loving, too wildly avenging
his Ilia's grief, he threw himself so far
wandering over the strict left bank where Jove
    never permitted.

They'll hear of it, our children, few as they are
because of their parents' sins, they'll hear of war
and citizens sharpening swords against citizens,
    not against Parthians.

What god can the people call as the Empire totters,
what prayer shall the virgin priestesses use to implore
Vesta, who leans away from their chants, and listens
    less and less?

cui dabit partes scelus expiandi
Iuppiter? Tandem venias, precamur,
nube candentes umeros amictus,
    augur Apollo;

sive tu mavis, Erycina ridens,
quam Iocus circum volat et Cupido;
sive neglectum genus et nepotes
    respicis, auctor,

heu nimis longo satiate ludo,
quem iuvat clamor galeaeque leves
acer et Mauri peditis cruentum
    vultus in hostem.

sive mutata iuvenem figura
ales in terris imitaris almae
filius Maiae, patiens vocari
    Caesaris ultor:

serus in caelum redeas, diuque
laetus intersis populo Quirini,
neve te nostris vitiis iniquum
    ocior aura

tollat; hic magnos potius triumphos,
hic ames dici pater atque princeps,
neu sinas Medos equitare inultos,
    te duce, Caesar.

What god will Jupiter choose to purify
our crimes? After so long, come down, Apollo,
prophetic god, we pray, your brilliant shoulders
    cloaked in cloud;

or should it be you, Venus of subtle laughter,
Joy and Arousal fluttering at your side;
or Mars, our ancestor, if you look on
    your neglected children,

you, gorged on this endless game of war, still thrilled
at battle clang and glare of helmets, the grim
face of the Moorish foot-soldier head to head
    with his enemy bleeding.

Or could it be you, sweet Maia's wing-footed child,
changed in your shape to act the part on earth
of a mortal young man, letting yourself be called
    Caesar's avenger:

don't hurry back to the heavens, be happy here
long years among Quirinus' people; don't
let some quick breeze snatch you away from us
    in your scorn of our vices;

here, on earth, may you love great victories,
here may you love us to call you Father and Princeps,
and don't let the Medes go on scot-free, raiding,
    while you lead us, Caesar.

                        Rosanna Warren

I.3

Sic te diva potens Cypri,
   sic fratres Helenae, lucida sidera,
ventorumque regat pater
   obstrictis aliis praeter Iapyga,

navis, quae tibi creditum
   debes Vergilium; finibus Atticis
reddas incolumem, precor,
   et serves animae dimidium meae.

illi robur et aes triplex
   circa pectus erat, qui fragilem truci
commisit pelago ratem
   primus, nec timuit praecipitem Africum

decertantem Aquilonibus
   nec tristes Hyadas nec rabiem Noti,
quo non arbiter Hadriae
   maior, tollere seu ponere volt freta.

quem mortis timuit gradum,
   qui siccis oculis monstra natantia,
qui vidit mare turbidum et
   infames scopulos, Acroceraunia?

nequiquam deus abscidit
   prudens Oceano dissociabili
terras, si tamen impiae
   non tangenda rates transiliunt vada.

audax omnia perpeti
   gens humana ruit per vetitum nefas.
audax Iapeti genus
   ignem fraude mala gentibus intulit.

I.3

I pray the goddess of Cyprus might,
    And those bright stars, Helen's brothers,
And the father of winds, impeding their flight—
    Not the Nor'wester's, but all the others'—

So steer this ship, trustworthy host
    Of precious Virgil, to bring him whole
And safe back from the Attic coast,
    And with him the other half of my soul!

A brass-bound heart of oak had he
    Who was the first to launch a frail
Craft upon the crafty sea
    Undaunted by a Southerly gale,

Contending with the North's erratic
    Blasts, or the rainy Hyades,
Or what frets and soothes the Adriatic
    Most, an arbitrary breeze.

Dreading imminent death, dry-eyed
    Watching wonders wandering under
The water, he recoiled from the roiling tide
    And those notorious rocks, The Cliffs of Thunder.

Though god divided, all in vain,
    These social lands from the watery waste,
Across the unavoidable main
    How many godless vessels haste!

Men, ready for anything, are quick
    Forbidden wickedness to find;
Prometheus by a dirty trick
    Brought ready fire to humankind.

post ignem aetheria domo
    subductum macies et nova febrium
terris incubuit cohors,
    semotique prius tarda necessitas

leti corripuit gradum.
    expertus vacuum Daedalus aëra
pinnis non homini datis;
    perrupit Acheronta Herculeus labor.

nil mortalibus ardui est;
    caelum ipsum petimus stultitia, neque
per nostrum patimur scelus
    iracunda Iovem ponere fulmina.

But after fire was brought down to earth
   From its heavenly haven, with it a corps
Of new diseases came, and dearth,
   So death, remote and slow before,

Sooner than necessary began.
   Daedalus dared thin air as well
On wings unnatural to man.
   Hercules broke the doors of hell.

Is nothing too forbidding now
   For mortals? Our folly scales the sky;
Our naughtiness will not allow
   Jove to lay his thunderbolts by.

Daryl Hine

I.4

Solvitur acris hiems grata vice veris et Favoni,
    trahuntque siccas machinae carinas,
ac neque iam stabulis gaudet pecus aut arator igni,
    nec prata canis albicant pruinis.

iam Cytherea choros ducit Venus imminente luna,
    iunctaeque Nymphis Gratiae decentes
alterno terram quatiunt pede, dum graves Cyclopum
    Volcanus ardens visit officinas.

nunc decet aut viridi nitidum caput impedire myrto
    aut flore, terrae quem ferunt solutae;
nunc et in umbrosis Fauno decet immolare lucis,
    seu poscat agna sive malit haedo.

pallida Mors aequo pulsat pede pauperum tabernas
    regumque turres. o beate Sesti,
vitae summa brevis spem nos vetat incohare longam.
    iam te premet nox fabulaeque Manes

et domus exilis Plutonia; quo simul mearis,
    nec regna vini sortiere talis,
nec tenerum Lycidan mirabere, quo calet iuventus
    nunc omnis et mox virgines tepebunt.

I.4

Winter's melting in the mild west wind;
time to haul the dry-docked boats to the shore.
The farmer has cabin fever; his pent-up flocks
are itching for the meadow, and the meadow's
greening already in its morning thaw.

Under a spring moon, Cytherean Venus
leads her dancing garland of Nymphs and Graces
hand in hand, light-footed, across the fields
while red-faced Vulcan fires up the lightning forge
and puts his lumbering Cyclopes through their paces.

Now's the time to crown your oil-slicked hair;
bind it with emerald myrtle or with quivers
of blossom freshly hatched from the ice-shelled earth;
now cut a throat for Faunus in the shadows;
a lamb or kid—whichever he prefers . . .

Death, pale and impartial, stands at the door;
enters with equal indifference the squatter's shack
and rich man's villa. Oh lucky Sestius!
Life's too short for all but the simplest dreams;
soon you'll be lodged in one of Pluto's black

airless rooms, where no one rolls the dice
to rule the revels, and no one gazes
at tender Lycidas, whom all the boys
lust after now, and all the girls will soon
be smothering with imaginary embraces.

James Lasdun

I.5

Quis multa gracilis te puer in rosa
perfusus liquidis urget odoribus
    grato, Pyrrha, sub antro?
        cui flavam religas comam,

simplex munditiis? heu quotiens fidem
mutatosque deos flebit et aspera
    nigris aequora ventis
        emirabitur insolens,

qui nunc te fruitur credulus aurea,
qui semper vacuam, semper amabilem
    sperat, nescius aurae
        fallacis. miseri, quibus

intemptata nites. me tabula sacer
votiva paries indicat uvida
    suspendisse potenti
        vestimenta maris deo.

I.5

What slip of a boy, all slick with what perfumes,
is pressing on you now, o Pyrrha, in
your lapping crannies, in your rosy rooms?

Who's caught up in your net today, your coil
of elegant coiffure? He'll call himself
a sucker soon enough, and often, and rail

at the breakers—God of his word, you of your faith.
The darkest sort of thought will fill his form
when breezes bristle, mirrors roughen—just you wait!

So far, his seas are barely stirred. You are forever
fair to his fairweather mind, and golden
to his gullibility: no storms are forecast there,

and no distress. What blind and wretched men—
you've barely touched them, yet they find you gripping!
Whereas I have tendered my last and best

regards to the Gods of the wave, as temple tablets
will attest. I've thrown off the habit, and hung up
my wet suit there. (You see? It's dripping.)

Heather McHugh

I.6

Scriberis Vario fortis et hostium
victor Maeonii carminis alite,
quam rem cumque ferox navibus aut equis
    miles te duce gesserit.

nos, Agrippa, neque haec dicere nec gravem
Pelidae stomachum cedere nescii
nec cursus duplicis per mare Vlixei
    nec saevam Pelopis domum

conamur, tenues grandia, dum pudor
imbellisque lyrae Musa potens vetat
laudes egregii Caesaris et tuas
    culpa deterere ingeni.

quis Martem tunica tectum adamantina
digne scripserit aut pulvere Troico
nigrum Merionen aut ope Palladis
    Tydiden superis parem?

nos convivia, nos proelia virginum
sectis in iuvenes unguibus acrium
cantamus, vacui, sive quid urimur,
    non praeter solitum leves.

I.6

Varius, a bard of Homeric sweep
will praise your valor and your victories,
all the daring feats of navy and cavalry
under your wise command.

No epic grandeur, Agrippa, will I attempt.
Achilles' moods and tantrums,
the wanderings of sly Ulysses,
and Pelops' house of horrors

are too lofty subjects for me. Modesty
and my unbelligerent Muse forbid me
to lessen Caesar's glory
and your own with my ineptitude.

What poet is good enough to depict
Mars in his adamantine armor?
Meriones begrimed in Trojan dust?
Diomedes squaring off against two gods?

Epic winefests are my specialty.
Virgins fighting off their beaus with nails clipped sharp
I celebrate in my carefree manner,
my heart at peace or fired up by a spark of love.

Charles Simic

I.7

Laudabunt alii claram Rhodon aut Mytilenen
  aut Ephesum bimarisve Corinthi
moenia vel Baccho Thebas vel Apolline Delphos
  insignes aut Thessala Tempe.

sunt quibus unum opus est, intactae Palladis urbem
  carmine perpetuo celebrare et
undique decerptam fronti praeponere olivam.
  plurimus in Iunonis honorem

aptum dicet equis Argos ditesque Mycenas.
  me nec tam patiens Lacedaemon
nec tam Larisae percussit campus opimae,
  quam domus Albuneae resonantis

et praeceps Anio ac Tiburni lucus et uda
  mobilibus pomaria rivis.
albus ut obscuro deterget nubila caelo
  saepe Notus neque parturit imbres

perpetuos, sic tu sapiens finire memento
  tristitiam vitaeque labores
molli, Plance, mero, seu te fulgentia signis
  castra tenent seu densa tenebit

Tiburis umbra tui. Teucer Salamina patremque
  cum fugeret, tamen uda Lyaeo
tempora populea fertur vinxisse corona,
  sic tristes adfatus amicos:

"quo nos cumque feret melior fortuna parente,
  ibimus, o socii comitesque!
nil desperandum Teucro deuce et auspice Teucro!
  certus enim promisit Apollo

I.7

Some celebrate Mytilene or shining Rhodes,
    Ephesus too, and Corinth's sea-lapped walls,
Thebes dear to Bacchus, or the Thessalian vale,
    and Delphi sacred to Apollo;

others incessantly and exclusively praise
    the city of virgin Pallas, weaving garlands
of olive leaves plucked from each and every tree;
    many in Juno's honor will sing

of Mycenae, or of Argos, famed for horses—
    let them! For me, not rude Sparta nor the plain
of rich Larisa compares with Albunea's
    echoing cavern, the turbulent

Anio, Tiburnus's grove, and the headlong creeks
    that water the orchards there. And just as Notus,
a clearing wind, purges the darkened sky of clouds,
    even when it is raining hardest,

so you, Plancus, will be wise to remember
    that this life's continual cares may be dispelled
by a good wine—whether you are in garrison
    among the gaudy pennants, or deep

in the shade of your own Tibur. Even Teucer,
    fleeing his father and his birthplace Salamis,
wreathed his brow with poplar leaves and, gulping wine,
    cheered his stricken comrades with these words:

"Wherever Fortune, a kinder father, may lead,
    never despair, but follow Teucer's auspices,
under Teucer's command: Apollo has promised
    another Salamis in a new land.

"ambiguam tellure nova Salamina futuram.
      o fortes peioraque passi
mecum saepe viri, nunc vino pellite curas;
      cras ingens iterabimus aequor."

Therefore, my brave heroes, who have so often borne
     far worse ordeals with me, let us drink deep of wine
and banish our cares. For tomorrow, once again,
     we set forth upon the mighty sea."

Richard Howard

I.8

Lydia, dic, per omnes
   te deos oro, Sybarin cur properes amando
perdere; cur apricum
   oderit campum, patiens pulveris atque solis;

cur neque militaris
   inter aequales equitet, Gallica nec lupatis
temperet ora frenis.
   cur timet flavum Tiberim tangere? cur olivum

sanguine viperino
   cautius vitat, neque iam livida gestat armis
bracchia, saepe disco,
   saepe trans finem iaculo nobilis expedito?

quid latet, ut marinae
   filium dicunt Thetidis sub lacrimosa Troiae
funera, ne virilis
   cultus in caedem et Lycias proriperet catervas?

I.8

In the name of all that's holy,
Lydia, why such determination
to break Sybaris

with love? Why has he left
the field after he'd been so patient
with dust and sun?

Why isn't he still with his peers,
testing his mettle as a soldier does,
using his spiked bit to rein in

his frenzied Gallic mount? Why is he now
afraid even to touch the yellow Tiber,
much less to bathe in it?

Why is he put off by the oil
used to grease the wrestler's body,
as if it were some snake's?

Where are the livid bruises
left by weapons on his own body,
this winner with the discus,

the javelin, who threw so often
so far past the mark? Why does he
hide himself as if he were Thetis' son,

whom she hid in guise of a girl, they say,
seeing the many dead of Troy
and the grief of the still living,

for fear that a manly appearance
might hurry him back
to the Lycian cohorts and the slaughter?

Robert Creeley

I.9

Vides ut alta stet nive candidum
Soracte, nec iam sustineant onus
   silvae laborantes, geluque
      flumina constiterint acuto?

dissolve frigus ligna super foco
large reponens atque benignius
   deprome quadrimum Sabina,
      o Thaliarche, merum diota.

permitte divis cetera, qui simul
stravere ventos aequore fervido
   deproeliantes, nec cupressi
      nec veteres agitantur orni.

quid sit futurum cras, fuge quaerere et
quem Fors dierum cumque dabit, lucro
   appone nec dulces amores
      sperne puer neque tu choreas,

donec virenti canities abest
morosa. nunc et campus et areae
   lenesque sub noctem susurri
      composita repentantur hora,

nunc et latentis proditor intumo
gratus puellae risus ab angulo
   pignusque dereptum lacertis
      aut digito male pertinaci.

I.9

See how Soracte, glistening, stands out high in
its cape of snow, how laboring woods let go of
    their load, and all the streams are frozen
        over completely with sharpest cold now.

Undo the chill by piling the logs up high on
the hearth, and be most generous, too, in drawing
    the undiluted drink four winters
        old, Thaliarchus, from Sabine wine jars.

Entrust, then, all the rest to the Gods: as soon as
they've calmed the winds that battle across the plain of
    the turbid sea, the cypresses and
        ash trees of old will no longer tremble.

Avoid inquiring too what will come tomorrow
and enter a credit line for every day that
    is handed you by Fortune: never
        pass up sweet love or the lovely dancing,

while you're yet young and vigorous, irritable
old age yet distant, seek out the Field of Mars and
    the public squares at trysting-time when
        whisperings surface as night comes on, and

now the telltale laugh of a lurking girl in
a darkened corner just as some ring or bracelet
    is being snatched from off an arm or
        finger that almost seems unresisting.

                     John Hollander

I. 10

Mercuri, facunde nepos Atlantis,
qui feros cultus hominum recentum
voce formasti catus et decorae
    more palaestrae,

te canam, magni Iovis et deorum
nuntium curvaeque lyrae parentem,
callidum, quicquid placuit, iocoso
    condere furto.

te, boves olim nisi reddidisses
per dolum amotas, puerum minaci
voce dum terret, viduos pharetra
    risit Apollo.

quin et Atridas duce te superbos
Ilio dives Priamus relicto
Thessalosque ignes et iniqua Troiae
    castra fefellit.

tu pias laetis animas reponis
sedibus virgaque levem coerces
aurea turbam, superis deorum
    gratus et imis.

I. 10

O Mercury, well-spoken grandson of Atlas,
you who civilized the first men, who gave them
speech and explained to them the rules of wrestling,
    I sing your praise;

O messenger of Jupiter and the other gods,
you the shrewd inventor of the curving lyre,
you with quick hands lifting what you like
    and hiding it away,

just after you were born, you stole Apollo's
cattle, and Apollo with a threatening voice
ordered them returned, then had to laugh
    when it dawned on him

you had swiped his quiver too. You slipped Priam
with his riches out of Troy, managing to get
him past the Thessalian watchfires and past
    the enemy Greek camp.

You lead the pious dead to the place of bliss,
shepherding the ghostly crowd with your golden
staff. You move with ease among the gods
    above and those below.

Mark Strand

I.11

Tu ne quaesieris—scire nefas—quem mihi, quem tibi
finem di dederint, Leuconoë, nec Babylonios
temptaris numeros. ut melius, quicquid erit, pati!
seu plures hiemes, seu tribuit Iuppiter ultimam,
quae nunc oppositis debilitat pumicibus mare
Tyrrhenum. sapias, vina liques, et spatio brevi
spem longam reseces. dum loquimur, fugerit invida
aetas: carpe diem, quam minimum credula postero.

I.11

Don't ask, Clarice, we're not supposed to know
what end the gods intend for us.
Take my advice: don't gamble so
on horoscopes of Babylon. Far better just

to take what heaven might allot us, whether
it's winters galore, and more, until we're stiff,
or only this one wintertime to end all others,
grinding the Tuscany Sea with its pumice of cliff.

Get wise. Get wine, and one good filter for it.
Cut that high hope down to size, and pour it
into something fit for men. Think less
of more tomorrows, more of this

one second, endlessly unique: it's
jealous, even as we speak, and it's
about to split again . . .

Heather McHugh

Quem virum aut heroa lyra vel acri
tibia sumis celebrare, Clio?
quem deum? cuius recinet iocosa
   nomen imago

aut in umbrosis Heliconis oris
aut super Pindo gelidove in Haemo,
unde vocalem temere insecutae
   Orphea silvae,

arte materna rapidos morantem
fluminum lapsus celeresque ventos,
blandum et auritas fidibus canoris
   ducere quercus?

quid prius dicam solitis parentis
laudibus, qui res hominum ac deorum,
qui mare et terras variisque mundum
   temperat horis?

unde nil maius generatur ipso,
nec viget quicquam simile aut secundum
proximos illi tamen occupavit
   Pallas honores,

proeliis audax; neque te silebo,
Liber, et saevis inimica virgo
beluis, nec te, metuende certa
   Phoebe sagitta.

dicam et Alciden puerosque Ledae,
hunc equis, illum superare pugnis
nobilem; quorum simul alba nautis
   stella refulsit,

I.12

What man or hero—or what god shall I
Tune my flute, aim my lyre at, Clio,
And leave the sportive echoes in the sky?
Over the tracts of Helicon let it go,
That name, past Pindus and above the top
Of icy Haemus, or where Orpheus taught
Whole woods to dance, the rivercourse to stop
And, winding winds into the shape of song,
Gave ears to oaks. First let my praise belong
To Jove who shaped the earth, each sea and season,
To whom none can approach comparison.
Only Minerva earns a second place
In the celestial hierarchy—she
Followed by Diana's archery.
Yet Bacchus, too, claims praise for combat,
Come the arrows of Phoebus after that.
Castor and Pollux, Hercules, crowd the list—
Those two twins engineer both war and peace,
Their constellation rises above the sea
And, in its beam, the troubled surges fall
Below the rocks, the threatening breakers cease.

defluit saxis agitatus umor,
concidunt venti fugiuntque nubes,
et minax, quod sic voluere, ponto
    unda recumbit.

Romulum post hos prius an quietum
Pompili regnum memorem an superbos
Tarquini fasces, dubito, an Catonis
    nobile letum.

Regulum et Scauros animaeque magnae
prodigum Paulum, superante Poeno,
gratus insigni referam camena
    Fabriciumque.

hunc et intonsis Curium capillis
utilem bello tulit et Camillum
saeva paupertas et avitus apto
    cum lare fundus.

crescit occulto velut arbor aevo
fama Marcelli; micat inter omnes
Iulium sidus, velut inter ignes
    luna minores.

gentis humanae pater atque custos,
orte Saturno, tibi cura magni
Caesaris fatis data: tu secundo
    Caesare regnes.

ille seu Parthos Latio imminentes
egerit iusto domitos triumpho,
sive subiectos Orientis orae
    Seras et Indos,

te minor latum reget aequus orbem:
tu gravi curru quaties Olympum,
tu parum castis inimica mittes
    fulmina lucis.

46

And then? Shall I recall the reign of Numa
Or turn to Romulus, or Brutus sing,
Who left Rome free once more, or Cato's death
Or all that string of heroes still left listening
To catch the echoes of their names? The farm
Passed on down generations, household gods,
And thrift brought us our heroes against harm
Seasoned by their virtuous poverty.
Marcellus' fame keeps growing like a tree
In silence and the Julian star glows on,
Leading all lesser lights, another moon.
May Jove whom Saturn, both a god and king,
Bestowed on Rome, keep Caesar in his care
Who'll show the Romans what they were and are:
For he'll not scorn an empire once possessed,
Reverting now to tribe and private war-chest,
Or heed directives from a lesser nation,
Drown all distinctions in a single notion.
O may divinity keep whole his thoughts
Against the murrain that abstraction yields
And Jove's own lightnings strike polluted fields.

Charles Tomlinson

I.13

Cum tu, Lydia, Telephi
   cervicem roseam, cerea Telephi
laudas bracchia, vae, meum
   fervens difficili bile tumet iecur.

tunc nec mens mihi nec color
   certa sede manet, umor et in genas
furtim labitur, arguens
   quam lentis penitus macerer ignibus.

uror, seu tibi candidos
   turparunt umeros immodicae mero
rixae, sive puer furens
   impressit memorem dente labris notam.

non, si me satis audias,
   speres perpetuum dulcia barbare
laedentem oscula, quae Venus
   quinta parte sui nectaris imbuit.

felices ter et amplius,
   quos inrupta tenet copula nec malis
divulsus querimoniis
   suprema citius solvet amor die.

I.13

Lydia, when you blither about his rosy throat
Or swoon at the sight of the pale white arms of Telephus,
Raving to *me,* I boil with bile.

My altered color tells my jealousy of Telephus,
And one furtive tear steals down my cheek
Revealing the heat which devastates my heart.

Did that young brute bruise your ivory shoulder
After too much to drink, or lustfully bite your lip
Moistened by Venus with her precious nectar?

If you paid attention to me you'd no longer desire
An oaf whose caresses pain you,
Who profanes your purity, who one day will betray you.

Remember, those are triply blessed who keep the faith
With a mature love, never marred by violence,
Existing peacefully, parted only by death.

Carolyn Kizer

I. 14

O navis, referent in mare te novi
fluctus. o quid agis! fortiter occupa
    portum. nonne vides, ut
        nudum remigio latus

et malus celeri saucius Africo
antemnaeque gemant, ac sine funibus
    vix durare carinae
        possint imperiosius

aequor? non tibi sunt integra lintea,
non di, quos iterum pressa voces malo.
    quamvis Pontica pinus,
        silvae filia nobilis,

iactes et genus et nomen inutile:
nil pictis timidus navita puppibus
    fidit. tu, nisi ventis
        debes ludibrium, cave.

nuper sollicitum quae mihi taedium,
nunc desiderium curaque non levis,
    interfusa nitentes
        vites aequora Cycladas.

I.14

O ship, a ground swell threatens
to set you adrift—look out!
Hurry to reach the harbor—no, don't stop
to look, but you've lost your oars.

The mast has snapped, sails slap at the wind,
your hull needs rope to tie it back together,
canvas has torn, but you no longer
have gods to get you out of trouble.

Though you're built of the best pine
from the most noble forest, upon a plank
of which your famous name is lettered—
and so beautifully—who can trust paint?

You make a sailor nervous. Be careful
or you'll become a toy of the storm.
You who, not that long ago, were just
my headache, my pain in the neck,

but who now have my heart aboard,
steer clear of those narrow seas
that cut past the bright lights
marking the rocks of the Cyclades.

Debora Greger

Pastor cum traheret per freta navibus
Idaeis Helenen perfidus hospitam,
ingrato celeres obruit otio
    ventos, ut caneret fera

Nereus fata: "mala ducis avi domum,
quam multo repetet Graecia milite,
coniurata tuas rumpere nuptias
    et regnum Priami vetus.

eheu, quantus equis, quantus adest viris
sudor! quanta moves funera Dardanae
genti! iam galeam Pallas et aegida
    currusque et rabiem parat.

nequicquam Veneris praesidio ferox
pectes caesariem grataque feminis
imbelli cithara carmina divides;
    nequicquam thalamo graves

hastas et calami spicula Cnosii
vitabis strepitumque et celerem sequi
Aiacem: tamen, heu serus! adulteros
    crines pulvere collines.

non Laërtiaden, exitium tuae
gentis, non Pylium Nestora respicis?
urgent impavidi te Salaminius
    Teucer, te Sthenelus, sciens

I. 15

While the young herdsman, Paris, a herdsman as faithless as he was fair,
was hauling Helen back on his boat
of Trojan pine, the sea-god Nereus would stop the sea-airs
that can't abide being stopped and float

this vision of the future: "It doesn't bode well that you've taken on deck
a woman whom the Greeks will band together and swear on oath
to recover by force, determined as they'll be to wreck
your marriage and old Priam's kingdom both,

and I dread to think of the sweat-drenched horses, the men drenched
    with sweat,
dread to think of the carnage
you're visiting on Troy. Even now Athena is laying out her breastplate and
    helmet,
limbering up her battle-carriage and battle-rage.

However confident you may be about coming under Venus's special care,
there'll be no point in pretending to groom
your long hair while from your measured lyre you pluck the measured airs
the ladies seem to go for. There'll be no point in hiding out in the
    bedroom

to avoid the heavy throwing-spears and Cretan arrowheads,
what with Ajax hard on your heels, what with the rumpus and ruck
of battle. Then you may dread
to think, after all, of your long hair dragged through the muck.

Can't you make out Ulysses, sworn enemy of your people, at your back?
Nestor of Pylos coming after you?
Teucer of Salamis hot on your tracks?
Not to speak of Sthenelus, who knows a thing or two

pugnae, sive opus est imperitare equis,
non auriga piger. Merionen quoque
nosces. ecce furit te reperire atrox
    Tydides melior patre,

quem tu, cervos uti vallis in altera
visum parte lupum graminis immemor,
sublimi fugies mollis anhelitu,
    non hoc pollicitus tuae.

iracunda diem proferet Ilio
matronisque Phrygum classis Achillei;
post certas hiemes uret Achaicus
    ignis Pergameas domos."

about handling himself in a fight, not to speak
of handling a chariot team.
Meriones is yet another Greek
with whom you'll be all too familiar. Diomedes also, whom some deem

deadlier than his father, Tydeus, is following in your wake,
and when you sight him, like a stag sighting a wolf on the opposite
    hillside,
you'll soon forget grass-nibbling and take off, head thrown back,
    breathless, all aquake—
hardly what she thought was coming to her, your bride.

For though Achilles and his fleet, consumed as they are with ire,
may delay the course of events, by the time ten years have rolled round
the Greeks will have set the fire
that will burn Troy to the ground."

Paul Muldoon

I.16

O matre pulchra filia pulchrior,
quem criminosis cumque voles modum
   pones iambis, sive flamma
      sive mari libet Hadriano.

non Dindymene, non adytis quatit
mentem sacerdotum incola Pythius,
   non Liber aeque, non acuta
      sic geminant Corybantes aera,

tristes ut irae, quas neque Noricus
deterret ensis nec mare naufragum
   nec saevus ignis nec tremendo
      Iuppiter ipse ruens tumultu.

fertur Prometheus addere principi
limo coactus particulam undique
   desectam et insani leonis
      vim stomacho apposuisse nostro.

irae Thyesten exitio gravi
stravere et altis urbibus ultimae
   stetere causae, cur perirent
      funditus imprimeretque muris

hostile aratrum exercitus insolens.
compesce mentem: me quoque pectoris
   temptavit in dulci iuventa
      fervor et in celeres iambos

misit furentem; nunc ego mitibus
mutare quaero tristia, dum mihi
   fias recantatis amica
      opprobriis animumque reddas.

I. 16

About my angry lines, burn them, do
Whatever you wish, or dip them
In the Adriatic Ocean; do this, hear me,
Handsome mother of a still more handsome daughter.

You know that what most disturbs the soul
Is not Dindymene, nor that one who lives
With the Great Snake, nor the half-
Mad dancers with their crying metals,

It is grim-faced anger. The Noric swords
Cannot dissolve it, nor the ship-
Swallowing sea, nor greedy fire, nor
God himself when he comes roaring down. . . .

Prometheus did what he did, he added a bit
To us from seals and orioles, dropped
Those bits into our clay, and had no choice
But to put into us the lion's mad angers. . . .

Anger is what broke Thyestes' life,
And many shining cities went down brick
By brick before anger, and aggressive
Battalions ran their ploughs in great

Delight over ground covering those walls.
Calm your mind. Heat tempted
Me in my sweet early days, and sent
Me deeply mad to one-sided poems. Now

I want to replace those sour lines with
Sweet lines; now, having sworn off harsh
Attacks, I want you to become
My friend, and give me back my heart.

Robert Bly

I.17

Velox amoenum saepe Lucretilem
mutat Lycaeo Faunus et igneam
    defendit aestatem capellis
        usque meis pluviosque ventos.

impune tutum per nemus arbutos
quaerunt latentes et thyma deviae
    olentis uxores mariti,
        nec virides metuunt colubras

nec Martialis haediliae lupos,
utcumque dulci, Tyndari, fistula
    valles et Vsticae cubantis
        levia personuere saxa.

di me tuentur, dis pietas mea
et Musa cordi est. hic tibi copia
    manabit ad plenum benigno
        ruris honorum opulenta cornu.

hic in reducta valle Caniculae
vitabis aestus, et fide Teia
    dices laborantis in uno
        Penelopen vitreamque Circen;

hic innocentis pocula Lesbii
duces sub umbra, nec Semeleius
    cum Marte confundet Thyoneus
        proelia, nec metues protervum

suspecta Cyrum, ne male dispari
incontinentes iniciat manus
    et scindat haerentem coronam
        crinibus immeritamque vestem.

I. 17

The goat-footed god, whenever exchanging his hill
for visits here, makes sure my flocks escape
the Dog Star's brutal summer sun and squalls;

he keeps the she-goats safe from the rancid male
to forage the forest for tender herbs and grasses,
their young unafraid of the packs of wolves or the snakes

as long as the Pan-flute pipes its pure sweet song
that cools and calms this copious green estate,
the song I spend my life and verse to sing.

You would be safe here too, to sing love songs,
Penelope and Circe both enthralled,
to sip mild wine in the shade in your gossamer dress,

miles away from the strife of gods and men,
miles away from your rash, possessive husband,
his hot breath in your hair, his groping hands.

Ellen Bryant Voigt

I. 18

Nullam, Vare, sacra vite prius severis arborem
circa mite solum Tiburis et moenia Catali;
siccis omnia nam dura deus proposuit neque
mordaces aliter diffugiunt sollicitudines.
quis post vina gravem militiam aut pauperiem crepat?
quis non te potius, Bacche pater, teque, decens Venus?
ac ne quis modici transiliat munera Liberi,
Centaurea monet cum Lapithis rixa super mero
debellata, monet Sithoniis non levis Euhius,
cum fas atque nefas exiguo fine libidinum
discernunt avidi. non ego te, candide Bassareu,
invitum quatiam nec variis obsita frondibus
sub divum rapiam. saeva tene cum Berecyntio
cornu tympana, quae subsequitur caecus Amor sui
et tollens vacuum plus nimio Gloria verticem
arcanique Fides prodiga, perlucidior vitro.

I. 18

Varsus: First plant your grapes. Not even trees suit your best soil so
    well—
sun-warmed riverine earth, under old walls, out of the wind. So will
your vines honor the Lord Bacchus who grants drought to the dry but
    lends
ease, brief ease, from the sharp bite of distress. Given wine, who
    complains?
Who'd waste breath on war tales or poverty? Instead we speak in words
that praise Bacchus the generous, and fairest Venus, decorus.
We keep our wits, too, thus praising the gift gods have made ripe for us.
We are warned by tales of how Centaurs and Lapiths brawled and died,

how Bacchus warned Sithonians in vain, when drunk lust mapped their
    path
between lawless and lawful desire. Never will I, brightest Lord,
provoke you or expose to air what you use thick leaves to conceal.
May no drums or Berecyntian hornpipes pulse to confuse us,
with blind Self-Love in their wake, and Ambition with empty head
    perched high—
and Faith who was once trusted with secrets turns into Faithlessness,
babbling everything anyhow anywhere, transparent as glass.

Marie Ponsot

I. 19

Mater saeva Cupidinum
  Thebanaeque iubet me Semelae puer
et lasciva Licentia
  finitis animum reddere amoribus.

urit me Glycerae nitor,
  splendentis Pario marmore purius;
urit grata protervitas
  et vultus nimium lubricus aspici.

in me tota ruens Venus
  Cyprum deseruit, nec patitur Scythas
et versis animosum equis
  Parthum dicere, nec quae nihil attinent.

hic vivum mihi caespitem, hic
  verbenas, pueri, ponite turaque
bimi cum patera meri:
  mactata veniet lenior hostia.

I.19

Desires' cruel Mother, together
with the son of Theban Semele
and ever lascivious Wantonness,

call me back to love's echoes
I had thought were ended. So
does Glycera incite me, the gloss

of her white skin like Parian marble,
her amorous forwardness,
her delicious face, turn me to aching.

Venus, deserting Cyprus, attacks with all her powers.
She will not let me talk of Scythians,
of Parthian horsemen fighting fiercely in retreat.

Naught but Love's subjects she permits.
So here, slaves, make a ritual place—
prepare the living greensward, scatter incense,

pour new wine in a bowl.
I'll sacrifice the animal required. May it lessen
the imperious impact of her arrival.

Robert Creeley

I. 20

Vile potabis modicis Sabinum
cantharis, Graeca quod ego ipse testa
conditum levi, datus in theatro
    cum tibi plausus,

care Maecenas eques, ut paterni
fluminis ripae simul et iocosa
redderet laudes tibi Vaticani
    montis imago.

Caecubum et prelo domitam Caleno
tum bibes uvam; mea nec Falernae
temperant vites neque Formiani
    pocula colles.

I.20

Your wine will be the ordinary Sabine
out of plain cups but I sealed it myself
in Greek wine jars and stored it on the day
   the theater thundered

for you, dear noble Maecenas, so the banks
of your native river and the Vatican
hill returned the happy repetition
   upon your recovery.

You can drink Caecuban and Calenian
vintages when you please, but my cups do not
know the taste of Falernian vineyards
   or Formian hillsides.

W. S. Merwin

I.21

Dianam tenerae dicite virgines,
intonsum, pueri, dicite Cynthium
    Latonamque supremo
      dilectam penitus Iovi.

vos laetam fluviis et nemorum coma,
quaecumque aut gelido prominet Algido,
    nigris aut Erymanthi
      silvis aut viridis Cragi;

vos Tempe totidem tollite laudibus
natalemque, mares, Delon Apollinis,
    insignemque pharetra
      fraternaque umerum lyra.

hic bellum lacrimosum, hic miseram famem
pestemque a populo et principe Caesare in
    Persas atque Britannos
      vestra motus aget prece.

I.21

Let the girls sing of Diana in joyful praise
And the boys of her twin, Apollo unshorn, shall sing
And honor their sacred mother, whom Jupiter, king
Of gods, so favored, honor with song and the bays.

Of Diana let the girls sing, goddess of streams
Who loves the icy mountain, the darkened leafage
Of the Erymanthian woods, the brighter boscage
Of Lycian heights, young girls, give her your hymns.

To Tempe, to Phoebus Apollo's native isle,
Give praise, you boys, and praise many times over
His broad shoulder slung with both quiver and lyre,
His brother's instrument, his festive, sacred soil.

Hearing your prayers Apollo, god-begotten,
Will ward off war and plague and all ill omen
From Caesar and his people, and banish famine
To the alien lands of Parthian and Briton.

Anthony Hecht

I.22

Integer vitae scelerisque purus
non eget Mauris iaculis neque arcu
nec venenatis gravida sagittis,
    Fusce, pharetra,

sive per Syrtes iter aestuosas
sive facturus per inhospitalem
Caucasum vel quae loca fabulosus
    lambit Hydaspes.

namque me silva lupus in Sabina,
dum meam canto Lalagen et ultra
terminum curis vagor expeditis,
    fugit inermem;

quale portentum neque militaris
Daunias latis alit aesculetis
nec Iubae tellus generat, leonum
    arida nutrix.

pone me pigris ubi nulla campis
arbor aestiva recreatur aura,
quod latus mundi nebulae malusque
    Iuppiter urget;

pone sub curru nimium propinqui
solis in terra domibus negata:
dulce ridentem Lalagen amabo,
    dulce loquentem.

I.22

The good man with a clear conscience
doesn't need the protection, Fusco,
of Moorish spears, nor arrows armed
    with poisoned tips,

even if he takes a dangerous journey
across the scorching Syrtes, or the forbidding
Caucasus, or by the distant river Indus,
    fearful in legend.

One day, when I left the Sabine farm—
avoiding my usual paths, unarmed,
carefree and singing of my Lalage—a wolf
    bolted away from me,

a monstrous predator more terrifying
than the beasts bred in the forest
of fierce Apulia, or the lions of Namibia
    that the desert feeds.

If I should be set down in an icy plain
—no trees swaying, no breezes—
with mists darkening the barren land
    that Jupiter despises,

or if I were stranded where no one can live,
because the sun rides so close to the earth,
I would keep on loving my dear Lalage,
    her laughter and love-talk.

                        Donald Hall

I.23

Vitas hinnuleo me similis, Chloë,
quaerenti pavidam montibus aviis
  matrem non sine vano
    aurarum et siluae metu.

nam seu mobilibus veris inhorruit
adventus foliis, seu virides rubum
  dimovere lacertae,
    et corde et genibus tremit.

atqui non ego te tigris ut aspera
Gaetulusve leo frangere persequor:
  tandem desine matrem
    tempestiva sequi viro.

You dash from my sight, little Chloë, the way, with fear,
a stray fawn bolts from path to bush in search
of her lost mother, trembling utterly at each
sweet nothing of the woods, each stir of air.

Let any thorn tree spring the briefest leaf,
let any lizard make the least green streak
toward any under-tangle—and she'll freeze,
blood knocking, heart at her knees.

But I'm no predatory cur, no wildcat appetite,
to track a baby down and eat her up. I'm only
human: I'm a man. The time is right, in you, for some
bold move. Now let your mother go. Now, let me come.

Heather McHugh

I. 24

Quis desiderio sit pudor aut modus
tam cari capitis? praecipe lugubres
cantus, Melpomene, cui liquidam pater
    vocem cum cithara dedit.

ergo Quintilium perpetuus sopor
urget? cui Pudor et Iustitiae soror,
incorrupta Fides, nudaque Veritas,
    quando ullum inveniet parem?

multis ille bonis flebilis occidit,
nulli flebilior quam tibi, Vergili.
tu frustra pius heu non ita creditum
    poscis Quintilium deos.

quid, si Threicio blandius Orpheo
auditam moderere arboribus fidem?
num vanae redeat sanguis imagini,
    quam virga semel horrida,

non lenis precibus fata recludere,
nigro compulerit Mercurius gregi?
durum: sed levius fit patientia,
    quicquid corrigere est nefas.

A dear friend gone: does grief require restraint?
Oh Muse of mourning, teach us a complaint,
Make music of our loss,
Sing in your clear sweet voice.

And so Quintilius sleeps perpetually.
When will integrity and loyalty
(Sister to justice), dignity, decorum
Find anyone to equal him?

His death was the occasion of a flood
Of tears. But he was never ours for good,
Virgil, so you weep and sob in vain;
He can't come back again.

Even were you to play with greater grace
Than Orpheus, whose lyre enchanted trees,
No life blood would flow back
Into the empty shade, once the grim crook

Of the soul-shepherd god had forced it in
To huddle with the rest in his dark pen.
Yes, it is hard. But patiently
Is the best way of bearing what must be.

Rachel Hadas

I.25

Parcius iunctas quatiunt fenestras
ictibus crebris iuvenes protervi,
nec tibi somnos adimunt, amatque
    ianua limen,

quae prius multum facilis movebat
cardines. audis minus et minus iam:
"me tuo longas pereunte noctes,
    Lydia, dormis?"

invicem moechos anus arrogantes
flebis in solo levis angiportu,
Thracio bacchante magis sub inter-
    lunia vento,

cum tibi flagrans amor et libido,
quae solet matres furiare equorum,
saeviet circa iecur ulcerosum,
    non sine questu,

laeta quod pubes hedera virenti
gaudeat pulla magis atque myrto,
aridas frondes hiemis sodali
    dedicet Euro.

I.25

How seldom now the shutters rattle
    with your lovers' shouts;
how rarely do you lose your sleep
    to hot young blood and clamor.
The very door that willingly
    indulged their ins and outs
is nowadays of still and stiller
    liminals enamored.

Almost never now the strains
    of that old hue and cry,
the compliment of their complaint
    in suitor singy-songing:
"O Lydia, my Lydia,
    you have to tell me why
you sleep so deep while I must die
    the whole night long, of longing."

You're getting yours. You'll suffer sure
    (a crone alone bewailing
some bad abandoner's hauteur,
    at some back alley railing—
north wind everywhere, no moon—
    but you all fever-struck
by bolts of heat so mean they'd make
    the mildest broodmare buck).

And there you'll stay, replaying moans
    at those young men who troop
toward myrtle's midnight glow of tones,
    or ivy bright with life,
while your leaves droop with envy's own
    unenviable blight—
consigned to any wind that stoops
    to winter, for a wife.

Heather McHugh

I.26

Musis amicus tristitiam et metus
tradam protervis in mare Creticum
    portare ventis, quis sub Arcto
        rex gelidae metuatur orae,

quid Tiridaten terreat, unice
securus. o quae fontibus integris
    gaudes, apricos necte flores,
        necte meo Lamiae coronam,

Pimplei dulcis. nil sine te mei
prosunt honores: hunc fidibus novis,
    hunc Lesbio sacrare plectro
        teque tuasque decet sorores.

I.26

Being cherished by the Muses, I'll appeal to
The winds to carry my melancholies off
To the seas of Crete. Which bearded German king,
Looking up at the Great Bear, worries us, or what disaster

Threatens Tiridates in Persia, it's all
One with me. Giver of new poems,
Lover of the clear springs, weave some
Ornate lines as a gift for Lucius.

If you don't come, none of my honoring
Will take hold. Let's do this in Alcaic meter,
With its sonorities; you and your sisters, do
Come, let's make this companion immortal.

Robert Bly

I.27

Natis in usum laetitiae scyphis
pugnare Thracum est: tollite barbarum
   morem, verecundumque Bacchum
     sanguineis prohibete rixis.

vino et lucernis Medus acinaces
immane quantum discrepat: impium
   lenite clamorem, sodales,
     et cubito remanete presso.

vultis severi me quoque sumere
partem Falerni? dicat Opuntiae
   frater Megyllae, quo beatus
     vulnere, qua pereat sagitta.

cessat voluntas? non alia bibam
mercede. quae te cumque domat Venus,
   non erubescendis adurit
     ignibus ingenuoque semper

amore peccas. quicquid habes, age,
depone tutis auribus.—a miser,
   quanta laboras in Charybdi,
     digne puer meliore flamma!

quae saga, quis te solvere Thessalis
magus venenis, quis poterit deus?
   vix inligatum te triformi
     Pegasus expediet Chimaera.

I. 27

Only a Thracian goon would lurch from tippling
To brawling. Barbarians one and all. For our part
Let's preserve the rites of Bacchus, our seemly and civil
Devotions in the calm service of pleasure.
Good wine imbibed by lamplight has nothing to do
With bashed-in cups or swordplay. Subdue your clamor,
My friends, and use your well-connected elbows
For hoisting moderate drinks. You ask that I
Knock back my own full share of Falernian must.
Then let's hear Megylla's brother tell us who knocked him
All of a heap with the heavy weapons of bliss.
Suddenly tongue-tied? Well then, I'm swearing off,
Not a drop more. Those are my fixed conditions.
Whichever beauty it was that sent you reeling,
There's nothing to blush about, since you only go
For the classy and hightoned. Come on, just whisper
Her name in my ear.
                              O you poor silly kid,
You've bought yourself a regular Charybdis;
You deserve better. What can Thessalian spells,
Wizards or magic ointments do for you now?
Snagged by the tripartite, hybrid beast, Chimera,
Not even Bellerophon, mounted on Pegasus, could save you.

Anthony Hecht

I.28

Te maris et terrae numeroque carentis harenae
    mensorem cohibent, Archyta,
pulveris exigui prope litus parva Matinum
    munera, nec quicquam tibi prodest

aërias temptasse domos animoque rotundum
    percurrisse polum morituro.
occidit et Pelopis genitor, conviva deorum,
    Tithonusque remotus in auras

et Iovis arcanis Minos admissus, habentque
    Tartara Panthoiden iterum Orco
demissum, quamvis clipeo Troiana refixo
    tempora testatus nihil ultra

nervos atque cutem morti concesserat atrae,
    iudice te non sordidus auctor
naturae verique. sed omnes una manet nox,
    et calcanda semel via leti.

dant alios Furiae torvo spectacula Marti,
    exitio est avidum mare nautis;
mixta senum ac iuvenum densentur funera, nullum
    saeva caput Proserpina fugit.

Me quoque devexi rapidus comes Orionis
    Illyricis Notus obruit undis.
at tu, nauta, vagae ne parce malignus harenae
    ossibus et capiti inhumato

particulam dare: sic, quodcumque minabitur Eurus
    fluctibus Hesperiis, Venusinae
plectantur silvae te sospite, multaque merces,
    unde potest, tibi defluat aequo

I.28

Calibrator of the sea and earth, who counted
　　infinite grains, Archytas,

now you're honored by a dusting of flung sand, now
　　you're lightly buried near Matine.

So what good did it do to dare castles in the air
　　or double the cube,

how did it behoove you, when your brains
　　were death-bent from day one,

death-meant, that is, from birth. When Tantalus,
　　who was the guest of gods, lies dead,

and Minos, despite glimpses into Jove's arcanum,
　　died, and Tithonus retired

as the ghost of wind. Euphorbus went to hell,
　　and came back as Pythagoras,

who recognized and seized the shield
　　he'd carried

in his former life. This feat proved nothing
　　more than skin and bone

give way to death, since Pythagoras,
　　you'll admit,

was no mean appraiser of the nature of
　　What-Is.

Yet I believe a single night awaits us,
　　one and all, and death

is known by all and one but once.
　　The Furies donate some

to bitter shows of war; the famished sea
　　feeds on the drowning

sailor's wreck; the old, the young, close ranks,
　　cold-pressed by death,

ab Iove Neptunoque sacri custode Tarenti.
    neglegis immeritis nocituram
postmodo te natis fraudem committere? fors et
    debita iura vicesque superbae

te maneant ipsum: precibus non linquar inultis,
    teque piacula nulla resolvent.
quamquam festinas, non est mora longa; licebit
    iniecto ter pulvere curras.

and Proserpine must clip her lock, at last,
    from every head.

I, too, was seized, a twin of Orion,
    whose stars drown

in the Adriatic when the south winds rage.
    Sailor—that is, you

who scan these seas right now—don't withhold
    my bit of beach.

Be a friend and toss some sand, a fickle honorific,
    onto my head

and bones, now so exposed. Then, whatever
    ill winds nag the starblown seas

or flog the oaks, you'll be preserved, and a thousand
    profits will flow down

to you from Jove, the source of such, and be redoubled
    by Neptune, the protector

of our fair city, Tarentum. Think, too, how any wrong
    you do is visited

upon your children, swindling their innocence—
    now doesn't that give pause?

And, as luck would have it, fellow traveler,
    your debt of justice

could be subject to the same neglect
    one day: dismissed,

my case will never rest, no offering will acquit you.
    Although you're in a rush,

this won't take long; just grant me my three tosses of
    the dust before you dash.

Alice Fulton

83

Icci, beatis nunc Arabum invides
gazis et acrem militiam paras
   non ante devictis Sabaeae
      regibus, horribilique Medo

nectis catenas? quae tibi virginum
sponso necato barbara serviet?
   puer quis ex aula capillis
      ad cyathum statuetur unctis,

doctus sagittas tendere Sericas
arcu paterno? quis neget arduis
   pronos relabi posse rivos
      montibus et Tiberim reverti,

cum tu coëmptos undique nobilis
libros Panaeti, Socraticam et domum
   mutare loricis Hiberis,
      pollicitus meliora, tendis?

I.29

Iccius, are you eyeing the treasures
of Arabia, getting ready to battle
   the unconquered King of Sheba,
     hammering up some shackles

for the horrible Medes? Once you've killed
her lover, what wild girl will be your slave?
   And what boy—scented oils in his hair,
     taught to aim Scythian arrows

from his father's bow—will be
your precious cupbearer? Who'll be surprised
   if streams run uphill and the Tiber
     flows backward, if you—

who collected your beloved books everywhere,
your Plato and Panaetius, you who
   showed such promise—trade them in
     for a suit of Spanish armor?

Mark Doty

I.30

O Venus, regina Cnidi Paphique,
sperne dilectam Cypron et vocantis
ture te multo Glycerae decoram
    transfer in aedem.

fervidus tecum puer et solutis
Gratiae zonis properentque Nymphae
et parum comis sine te Iuventas
    Mercuriusque.

I.30

Oh Venus, Empress of Cnidos and Paphos,
tear yourself away, if you can, from Cypress,
and come where Glycera summons you with sweet
billows of incense.

Bring with you to her bower your amorous boy,
Graces in loosened negligees, Nymphets,
and Youth (who's entirely worthless without you),
oh, and Mercury too.

James Lasdun

I.31

Quid dedicatum poscit Apollinem
vates? quid orat, de patera novum
    fundens liquorem? non opimae
       Sardiniae segetes feraces,

non aestuosae grata Calabriae
armenta, non aurum aut ebur Indicum,
    non rura, quae Liris quieta
       mordet aqua taciturnus amnis.

premant Calena falce quibus dedit
Fortuna vitem, dives ut aureis
    mercator exsiccet culillis
       vina Syra reparata merce,

dis carus ipsis, quippe ter et quater
anno revisens aequor Atlanticum
    impune. me pascunt olivae,
       me cichorea levesque malvae.

frui paratis et valido mihi,
Latoe, dones et, precor, integra
    cum mente, nec turpem senectam
       degere nec cithara carentem.

I.31

What does a poet ask at the new temple
to Apollo, and pray to have when pouring
    new wine from the bowl? Not for the piled
        harvests of opulent Sardinia

nor the contented herds in the warm climate
of Calabria, nor Indian gold or
    ivory, nor fields that the Liris
        wears away softly with its wordless flow.

Let those for whom Fortune provided it use
the pruning knife of Cales so that the rich
    merchant may drink from a golden bowl
        wine paid for with trade goods from Syria.

The gods seem to love that man. Three or four times
a year he sails out onto the Atlantic
    and survives. My own fare of olives,
        endives and light mallow root suits me best.

Son of Latona, let me take pleasure in
what I have, keeping the health of my body
    and mind through a dignified old age,
        not lacking honor, or songs, to the end.

W. S. Merwin

I.32

Poscimur. siquid vacui sub umbra
lusimus tecum, quod et hunc in annum
vivat et plures, age dic Latinum,
    barbite, carmen,

Lesbio primum modulate civi,
qui ferox bello tamen inter arma,
sive iactatam religarat udo
    litore navim,

Liberum et Musas Veneremque et illi
semper haerentem puerum canebat,
et Lycum nigris oculis nigroque
    crine decorum.

o decus Phoebi et dapibus supremi
grata testudo Iovis, o laborum
dulce lenimen medicumque, salve
    rite vocanti!

I.32

This I pray:

if ever in shadowed
ease I made of song

something lasting for
this year, and more—

        come,
give me a Roman song,
my lyre, though Greek yourself,
first played by Alcaeus of Lesbos, who
though fierce in war,

all the same—whether
in arms or mooring his
sea-tossed ship
to a shore itself wet with sea—

would sing of Bacchus,
the Muses, Venus, her
son clinging always
to her—and of Lycus,
lovely man . . . dark-eyed, dark
hair . . .

   You are the glory of Apollo;
you find welcome at the table
of highest Jupiter himself.

Sweet drug,
cure for suffering,
whenever I pray for help—please,

help me.

             Carl Phillips

I. 33

Albi, ne doleas plus nimio memor
immitis Glycerae neu miserabiles
decantes elegos, cur tibi iunior
    laesa praeniteat fide.

insignem tenui fronte Lycorida
Cyri torret amor, Cyrus in asperam
declinat Pholoën: sed prius Apulis
    iungentur capreae lupis,

quam turpi Pholoë peccet adultero.
sic visum Veneri, cui placet impares
formas atque animos sub iuga aënea
    saevo mittere cum ioco.

ipsum me melior cum peteret Venus,
grata detinuit compede Myrtale
libertina, fretis acrior Hadriae
    curvantis Calabros sinus.

I.33

Don't mope and moan, o Albius,
that Glycera's unsweet,
or drone in dragging elegies
of how you can't compete
with the likes of white-hot youth, as he
    who broke her faith now strokes her knee.

Lycoris, too, her brow refined,
for lowly Cyrus burned;
but Cyrus finds himself inclined
to Pholoë in turn,
who craves his low-life just as much
    as deer desire a wolfish touch.

So Venus rules, whose sport and joke
it is to link the two
least likely loves beneath her yoke—
her court reports untrue
since form and feeling both are tried
    (as I myself have testified:

I had good reason but I found
no good escape. That's how
old slaves to future slaves are bound,
in pleasure's plight. And now
what blows I take!—a gale emphatic
    as any that rakes the Adriatic).

Heather McHugh

I.34

Parcus deorum cultor et infrequens,
insanientis dum sapientiae
   consultus erro, nunc retrorsum
      vela dare atque iterare cursus

cogor relictos: namque Diespiter,
igni corusco nubila dividens
   plerumque, per purum tonantes
      egit equos volucremque currum;

quo bruta tellus et vaga flumina
quo Styx et invisi horrida Taenari
   sedes Atlanteusque finis
      concutitur. valet ima summis

mutare et insignem attenuat deus,
obscura promens; hinc apicem rapax
   Fortuna cum stridore acuto
      sustulit, hic posuisse gaudet.

I.34

Lazy in praising or praying to any god
and madly rational, a clever captain
cruising the open seas of human thought,

now I must bring my vessel full about,
tack into port and sail back out again
on the route from which I strayed. For the God of Gods,

who slices through the storm with flashes of fire,
this time in a clear sky came thundering
with his storied horses and his chariot,

whereby the dumb dull earth and its fluttering streams—
and the River Styx, and the dreaded mouth of the cave
at the end of the world—were shaken. So the god

does have sufficient power after all
to turn the tables on both high and low,
the mighty humbled and the meek raised up—

with a swift hiss of her wings, Fortune swoops down,
pleased to place the crown on this one's head,
as she was pleased to snatch it away from that one.

Ellen Bryant Voigt

I.35

O diva, gratum quae regis Antium,
praesens vel imo tollere de gradu
   mortale corpus vel superbos
     vertere funeribus triumphos,

te pauper ambit sollicita prece
ruris colonus, te dominam aequoris,
   quicumque Bithyna lacessit
     Carpathium pelagus carina,

te Dacus asper, te profugi Scythae
urbesque gentesque et Latium ferox
   regumque matres barbarorum et
     purpurei metuunt tyranni,

iniurioso ne pede proruas
stantem columnam, neu populus frequens
   "ad arma" cessantes, "ad arma"
     concitet imperiumque frangat.

te semper anteit saeva Necessitas,
clavos trabales et cuneos manu
   gestans aëna, nec severus
     uncus abest liquidumque plumbum.

te Spes et albo rara Fides colit
velata panno, nec comitem abnegat,
   utcumque mutata potentis
     veste domos inimica linquis.

at vulgus infidum et meretrix retro
periura cedit, diffugiunt cadis
   cum faece siccatis amici,
     ferre iugum pariter dolosi.

I.35

O Goddess, ruling loveliest Antium, who
at any time can lift up our mortal bodies
   from low to high condition or can
      make a proud triumph a funeral service,

to you the poorest farmer addresses anxious
entreaties, you as sovereign of the ocean
   the sailor in his Bithynian ship who
      keeps on provoking Carpathian waters,

of you the roughest Dacian, the Scythian who
retreating, fights, and Latium the ferocious,
   and cities, tribes, peoples, mothers of the
      barbarous kings and empurpled tyrants—

in fear, all, lest your violent foot demolish
the standing column, lest the assembled mob cry
   "To arms! to arms!" inciting all the
      laggards and trash the rule of order.

Ahead of you moves always the savage goddess,
Necessity, who carries huge spikes and wedges
   in hands of bronze, tight, cruel clamps and
      lead in the form of the molten metal;

to you both Hope and Loyalty, all too rare, with
her hands enwrapped in white, are devoted, neither
   of them deserting you when, wearing
      mourning, offended, you leave great houses,

but all the faithless crowds and the lying harlots
will turn away, and friends will disperse, as soon as
   the wine-jars have been emptied, being
      far too deceitful to share our burdens.

serves iturum Caesarem in ultimos
orbis Britannos et iuvenum recens
   examen, Eois timendum
     partibus Oceanoque rubro.

eheu, cicatricum et sceleris pudet
fratrumque. quid nos dura refugimus
   aetas? quid intactum nefasti
     liquimus? unde manum iuventus

metu deorum continuit? quibus
pepercit aris? o utinam nova
   incude diffingas retusum in
     Massagetas Arabasque ferrum!

Preserve our Caesar, soon to confront the Britons,
most distant in the world from us, and preserve now
    our young recruits who frighten Eastern
        regions afar on the Red Sea's margins.

Alas, then for the shame of our scars, our crimes and
our brothers we have felled—and what did we shrink from?
    as hardened as we are, is there an
        evil untouched by us? and from what have

our young men kept their hands far away in fear of
the gods? what altars have they left unpolluted?
    O hammer out anew our blunted
        swords against Arabs and Massagetae!

John Hollander

I.36

Et ture et fidibus iuvat
   placare et vituli sanguine debito
custodes Numidae deos,
   qui nunc Hesperia sospes ab ultima

caris multa sodalibus,
   nulli plura tamen dividit oscula
quam dulci Lamiae, memor
   actae non alio rege puertiae

mutataeque simul togae.
   Cressa ne careat pulchra dies nota,
neu promptae modus amphorae,
   neu morem in Salium sit requies pedum,

neu multi Damalis meri
   Bassum Threicia vincat amystide.
neu desint epulis rosae
   neu vivax apium neu breve lilium;

omnes in Damalin putres
   deponent oculos, nec Damalis novo
divelletur adultero,
   lascivis hederis ambitiosior.

I.36

With incense, and some music,
and a sacrificial calf, let's thank the gods
who watched over N_____. He's safely home
from the far West, bringing kisses

for all his old friends, especially L_____,
his first, his oldest pal. How many years ago
did they have the same teacher?
They put on their first long togas together.

Don't forget to mark this day in red
on the calendar, or to show your devotion
to a jug of wine. Don't stop the wild dancing,
the kind they do down in S_____.

When it comes to the drinking contests,
don't let B_____ be outdrunk
by the not-so-dumb D_____.
And don't forget roses, and parsley—

which lasts—and lilies, which don't.
Let everyone swoon over D_____,
but she won't leave her new lover.
She'll be all over him like ivy.

Debora Greger

I.37

Nunc est bibendum, nunc pede libero
pulsanda tellus, nunc Saliaribus
   ornare pulvinar deorum
     tempus erat dapibus, sodales.

antehac nefas depromere Caecubum
cellis avitis, dum Capitolio
   regina dementes ruinas,
     funus et imperio parabat

contaminato cum grege turpium
morbo virorum, quidlibet impotens
   sperare fortunaque dulci
     ebria. sed minuit furorem

vix una sospes navis ab ignibus,
mentemque lymphatam Mareotico
   redegit in veros timores
     Caesar, ab Italia volantem

remis adurgens, accipiter velut
molles columbas aut leporem citus
   venator in campis nivalis
     Haemoniae, daret ut catenis

fatale monstrum. quae generosius
perire quaerens nec muliebriter
   expavit ensem nec latentes
     classe cita reparavit oras.

ausa et iacentem visere regiam
vultu sereno, fortis et asperas
   tractare serpentes, ut atrum
     corpore combiberet venenum,

deliberata morte ferocior;
saevis Liburnis scilicet invidens
   privata deduci superbo
     non humilis mulier triumpho.

Now it's time to drink, now loosen your shoes
and dance, now bring around elaborate couches
and set the gods a feast, my friends! Before,

the time wasn't right to pour the vintage wines,
not while that queen and her vile brood of advisors,
dizzy with desire and drunk on luck,
were busy in deluded plots against us.

What sobered her up was seeing her fleet on fire—
hardly a ship survived—nightmare she woke to
sending her fleeing, flying, from our shores,

Caesar at the oars in close pursuit—
the way the hawk harasses the helpless dove,
or the hunter the hare in the snow-packed open field—
intent on dragging the monster back in chains.

And yet the death that she resolved was grand:
a woman who did not shrink from the drawn blade,
who did not try to slip away and hide,

she looked straight at the palace now in ruins,
her face composed, and without blinking took
into her arms the scaly venomous snakes
in order to drink each drop of their black wine,

and by that cup this woman of such fierce pride
made the triumph hers: that she would die
not as a slave, and not as someone's prize.

Ellen Bryant Voigt

I.38

Persicos odi, puer, apparatus,
displicent nexae philyra coronae;
mitte sectari, rosa quo locorum
    sera moretur.

simplici myrto nihil adlabores
sedulus, cura: neque te ministrum
dedecet myrtus neque me sub arta
    vite bibentem.

I. 38

I hate all Persian filagree, my boy,
And garlands woven out of lime tree bark.
On no account are you to hunt up, for my sake,
   The late-blooming rose.

Plain myrtle will do nicely for a crown.
It's not unbecoming on you, as your pour,
Or on me as I sip a glass of cool wine
   In the arbor's shade.

Robert Hass

LIBER | BOOK II

II . 1

Motum ex Metello consule civicum
bellique causas et vitia et modos
   ludumque Fortunae gravesque
      principum amicitias et arma

nondum expiatis uncta cruoribus,
periculosae plenum opus aleae,
   tractas et incedis per ignes
      suppositos cineri doloso.

paulum severae Musa tragoediae
desit theatris: mox, ubi publicas
   res ordinaris, grande munus
      Cecropio repetes cothurno,

insigne maestis praesidium reis
et consulenti, Pollio, curiae,
   cui laurus aeternos honores
      Delmatico peperit triumpho.

iam nunc minaci murmure cornuum
perstringis auris, iam litui strepunt,
   iam fulgor armorum fugaces
      terret equos equitumque vultus.

audire magnos iam videor duces,
non indecoro pulvere sordidos,
   et cuncta terrarum subacta
      praeter atrocem animum Catonis.

Iuno et deorum quisquis amicior
Afris inulta cesserat impotens
   tellure, victorum nepotes
      rettulit inferias Iugurthae.

II.1

The civic fray since Metellus' consulship,
the reasons for the war, all its phases and
    mistakes, the lottery of Luck, the
  fatal alliances formed by great men,

with swords still stained by sad internecine blood:
such subjects subject to necessary risks
    you treat, tiptoeing round the fires that
  smoulder beneath a facade of ashes.

Let your strict Muse retire from the tragic stage
awhile; when you have put our political
    affairs in order, reaffirm your
  grandiose gift for poetic drama.

Distinguished mouthpiece of lacrimose litigants,
you ornament the Senate's debates as well.
    The bays from your Dalmatian triumph,
  Pollio, earned you eternal glory.

And even now our ears are assaulted by
your bull-horns' warning note as the bugles blare;
    the glare of armor frightens both the
  runaway horse and its pale-faced rider.

I imagine magnificent generals
besmirched by sordid dust—which is no disgrace—
    and all the earth subdued except the
  fiercely invincible soul of Cato.

Though Juno, with those deities favorable
to Africa, had left unavenged the land,
    she fetched the victors' grandsons as a
  funeral sacrifice to Jugurtha.

quis non Latino sanguine pinguior
campus sepulcris impia proelia
   testatur auditumque Medis
      Hesperiae sonitum ruinae?

qui gurges aut quae flumina lugubris
ignara belli! quod mare Dauniae
   non decoloravere caedes?
      quae caret ora cruore nostro?

sed ne relictis, Musa procax, iocis
Ceae retractes munera neniae,
   mecum Dionaeo sub antro
      quaere modos leviore plectro.

What field is not enriched by our Roman blood
with tombs that testify to unholy war?
        The noisy downfall of our Western
    homeland is audible even in Persia.

What ocean gorge, which rivers are ignorant
of gruesome war? What seawater has not been
        discolored by Italian slaughter?
    Is there a shore by our blood unsullied?

Before, glib muse, you jettison all your jests
to drone a dreary dirge like Simonides',
        with me in some lubricious grotto
    try a more frivolous kind of music.

Daryl Hine

II.2

Nullus argento color est avaris
abdito terris, inimice lamnae
Crispe Sallusti, nisi temperato
    splendeat usu.

vivet extento Proculeius aevo,
notus in fratres animi paterni:
illum aget pinna metuente solvi
    Fama superstes.

latius regnes avidum domando
spiritum, quam si Libyam remotis
Gadibus iungas et uterque Poenus
    serviat uni.

crescit indulgens sibi dirus hydrops,
nec sitim pellit, nisi causa morbi
fugerit venis et aquosus albo
    corpore languor.

redditum Cyri solio Phraaten
dissidens plebi numero beatorum
eximit Virtus populumque falsis
    dedocet uti

vocibus, regnum et diadema tutum
deferens uni propriamque laurum,
quisquis ingentes oculo inretorto
    spectat acervos.

II.2

You, Crispus Sallust, know how dull silver is,
kept idle in the greedy earth. And you know
how bravely it gleams when modestly deployed,
usable, useful.

Think of Proculeius. His fame will endure
thanks to his fathering care for his brothers.
Fame's unfaltering wings bear his acts aloft,
steadily soaring.

Freedom from avarice broadens your kingdom.
Even if Spain and Carthage—impossibly—
along with their peoples, were joined into one,
your realm is greater.

Dropsy and its signal thirst are doubled
by drinking. The watery-weak pale body
fights off that thirst best not by cool draughts but by
curing its causes.

Phraates got his throne back. But Virtue disdains
false names, does not hold him happy, and teaches
ordinary speech to prize truth in naming,
gladly conferring

laurels, crown, and powers of governance
on one who strolls past others' piled-up treasures
without greed, without a second glance,
envying no one.

Marie Ponsot

II.3

Aequam memento rebus in arduis
servare mentem, non secus in bonis
    ab insolenti temperatam
        laetitia, moriture Delli,

seu maestus omni tempore vixeris,
seu te in remoto gramine per dies
    festos reclinatum bearis
        interiore nota Falerni.

quo pinus ingens albaque populus
umbram hospitalem consociare amant
    ramis? quid obliquo laborat
        lympha fugax trepidare rivo?

huc vina et unguenta et nimium breves
flores amoenae ferre iube rosae,
    dum res et aetas et sororum
        fila trium patiuntur atra.

cedes coëmptis saltibus et domo
villaque, flavus quam Tiberis lavit,
    cedes, et exstructis in altum
        divitiis potietur heres.

divesne, prisco natus ab Inacho,
nil interest an pauper et infima
    de gente sub divo moreris;
        victima nil miserantis Orci.

omnes eodem cogimur, omnium
versatur urna serius ocius
    sors exitura et nos in aeternum
        exsilium impositura cumbae.

II.3

To keep the soul serene even when we come upon
The arduous, and yet remain moderately unmoved
When gifts roll in, well, that's my advice for you,
Friend Dellius, for you are mortal too.

Evenness is good, whether disasters make
Everything crooked, or whether you can enjoy
Sipping, while you lie on your back
In the grass, the host's hidden-away wine.

Why do the darkling pines and the white
Delicate poplars weave their shady
Branches together, and the excited water
Work to curl itself around us?

Bring us roses, already turning dark,
And cardamom and wines; being rich
And young, we must trust the dark threads
Of the Three Sisters are still unbroken.

You'll soon lose your cunningly acquired
Strips of woods, the estate by the yellow
Tiber, the Roman house, its silver and gold,
To some miserable heir, and it's over.

Whether descended from the great houses,
Or drifting unprotected under the naked
Sky, it's all one; we are sacrifices
To Death, not well-known for compassion.

We are obliged and herded. The lot is
Inside the urn; the ball with our number
Will roll out. And what we'll get
Is an everlasting absence from home.

Robert Bly

115

II.4

Ne sit ancillae tibi amor pudori,
Xanthia Phoceu. prius insolentem
serva Briseis niveo colore
    movit Achillem;

movit Aiacem Telamone natum
forma captivae dominum Tecmessae;
arsit Atrides medio in triumpho
    virgine rapta,

barbarae postquam cecidere turmae
Thessalo victore et ademptus Hector
tradidit fessis leviora tolli
    Pergama Grais.

nescias an te generum beati
Phyllidis flavae decorent parentes:
regium certe genus, et penates
    maeret iniquos.

crede non illam tibi de scelesta
plebe dilectam neque sic fidelem,
sic lucro aversam potuisse nasci
    matre pudenda.

bracchia et voltum teretesque suras
integer laudo; fuge suspicari,
cuius octavum trepidavit aetas
    claudere lustrum.

II.4

To love a slave girl, Xanthias,
Need cause you no embarrassment,
Heroes of Greek mythology
Furnish such ample precedent.

Achilles loved his serving maid
Briseis, snowy white;
And Ajax loved Tecmessa;
And one could also cite

Triumphant Agamemnon, hot
For a captive girl
When Hector's loss, Achilles' might
Shook Troy until it fell.

Your sweetheart's family may well be
Rich—you inherit in that case.
And they must be of royal blood,
Though fallen into some disgrace.

Your lady comes of noble stock,
For sure. What proletarian
Would show such loyalty, regard
Mere wealth with such disdain?

Her face, her arms, her lovely legs!
I praise these beauties with a clear
Conscience, beyond all reproach.
Please! I have passed my fortieth year.

Rachel Hadas

II.5

Nondum subacta ferre iugum valet
cervice, nondum munia comparis
    aequare nec tauri ruentis
        in venerem tolerare pondus.

circa virentes est animus tuae
campos iuvencae, nunc fluviis gravem
    solantis aestum, nunc in udo
        ludere cum vitulis salicto

praegestientis. tolle cupidinem
immitis uvae: iam tibi lividos
    distinguet autumnus racemos
        purpureo varius colore.

iam te sequetur (currit enim ferox
aetas, et illi, quos tibi dempserit,
    apponet annos), iam proterva
        fronte petet Lalage maritum,

dilecta, quantum non Pholoë fugax,
non Chloris, albo sic umero nitens,
    ut pura nocturno renidet
        luna mari Cnidiusve Gyges,

quem si puellarum insereres choro,
mire sagaces falleret hospites
    discrimen obscurum solutis
        crinibus ambiguoque vultu.

II. 5

She is still young, not ready for the yoke
of a marriage nor for dutiful housekeeping,
    not ready for the lust of the bull
        who rages to mount her.

As a heifer she contents herself grazing
among the green pleasures of a meadow,
    and in noon's heat she cools herself
        by wading in a stream.

She enjoys the sisterhood of other heifers
in the shade of a willow. Put away for now
    your desire for grapes not yet ripe.
        Soon yellow autumn will arrive

and the vine's clusters turn purple, luxurious
as they swell with juice. Then she will want you,
    and her youth extend over years,
        as yours diminishes.

Boldly, Lalage will pursue her husband. You'll take
more pleasure in her than you did in the coy Pholoë,
    or in Chloris whose white shoulders glimmered
        like the moon's swath on the sea,

or in beautiful Gyges of Cnidia, his hair
as long as a maid's. If he stood among women
    a stranger might be puzzled, pondering
        whether he was boy or girl.

Donald Hall

II.6

Septimi, Gadis aditure mecum et
Cantabrum indoctum iuga ferre nostra et
barbaras Syrtes, ubi Maura semper
    aestuat unda,

Tibur Argeo positum colono
sit meae sedes utinam senectae
sit modus lasso maris et viarum
    militiaeque.

unde si Parcae prohibent iniquae
dulce pellitis ovibus Galaesi
flumen et regnata petam Laconi
    rura Phalantho.

ille terrarum mihi praeter omnes
angulus ridet, ubi non Hymetto
mella decedunt viridique certat
    baca Venafro;

ver ubi longum tepidasque praebet
Iuppiter brumas, et amicus Aulon
fertili Baccho minimum Falernis
    invidet uvis.

ille te mecum locus et beatae
postulant arces; ibi tu calentem
debita sparges lacrima favillam
    vatis amici.

II.6

Septimius, who would go with me to Gades
and Cantabria, ignorant of our iron will,
to the barbarous Syrtes, where Moorish waves
    rage perpetually,

let Tibur, settled by the Argive,
be the scene of my retirement, my final
resting place when I'm exhausted by the sea,
    the road, and warfare.

And if the harsh Fates keep me from there,
I will seek the Galaesus's sweet waters, cherished
by its skin-cloaked sheep, and fields once ruled by
    Spartan Phalanthus.

You see, that patch of ground shines for me
over all others, where the honey yields nothing
to Hymettus, and the olives rival those
    of green Venafrum;

where Jupiter brings warm springs
and tepid winters, and Aulon, friend
to fertile Bacchus, barely envies Falernum's
    famed bunches of grapes.

That blissful place urges both of us
to its heights; and there you will sprinkle tears
of remembrance on the still warm ashes
    of your poet-friend.

                    John Kinsella

II.7

O saepe mecum tempus in ultimum
deducte Bruto militiae duce,
    quis te redonavit Quiritem
        dis patriis Italoque caelo,

Pompei, meorum prime sodalium,
cum quo morantem saepe diem mero
    fregi, coronatus nitentes
        malobathro Syrio capillos?

tecum Philippos et celerem fugam
sensi relicta non bene parmula,
    cum fracta Virtus et minaces
        turpe solum tetigere mento.

sed me per hostes Mercurius celer
denso paventem sustulit aëre;
    te rursus in bellum resorbens
        unda fretis tulit aestuosis.

ergo obligatam redde Iovi dapem,
longaque fessum militia latus
    depone sub lauru mea nec
        parce cadis tibi destinatis.

oblivioso levia Massico
ciboria exple, funde capacibus
    unguenta de conchis. quis udo
        deproperare apio coronas

curatve myrto? quem Venus arbitrum
dicet bibendi? non ego sanius
    bacchabor Edonis: recepto
        dulce mihi furere est amico.

II.7

So often with me then in the face of death,
Back when Brutus was our captain . . .
   And now at last, who's brought you
      Home to Italy, her gods, her skies?

O Pompey, old friend and first comrade,
Just remember how we used to drink
   The day long, leaves in our hair
      All slick with Syrian oils.

With you too I fought in Philippi,
Abandoning to my shame my shield
   In the rout, when courage failed
      And the brave were crushed underfoot.

But swift Mercury rescued me, in a thick fog
Sped me through the threatening troops,
   Even while a relentless wave of war
      Sucked you back under the bloody surf.

So render now the feast you pledged to Jove.
Rest your battle-wearied body here
   Under my laurel tree, and try
      The wine I've set apart for you.

Fill the polished goblet with intoxicating red.
Pour perfume from the brimming shells.
   Which of us will weave the garland
      Of myrtle and dew-damp parsley?

Which of us, by a throw of the dice,
Will first raise his cup to salute the other?
   I'll drink as in an orgy, thrilled
      To have regained my friend.

J. D. McClatchy

II.8

Ulla si iuris tibi peierati
poena, Barine, nocuisset umquam,
dente si nigro fieres vel uno
    turpior ungui,

crederem. sed tu simul obligasti
perfidum votis caput, enitescis
pulchrior multo iuvenumque prodis
    publica cura.

expedit matris cineres opertos
fallere et toto taciturna noctis
signa cum caelo gelidaque divos
    morte carentes.

ridet hoc, inquam, Venus ipsa; rident
simplices Nymphae ferus et Cupido,
semper ardentis acuens sagittas
    cote cruenta.

adde quod pubes tibi crescit omnis,
servitus crescit nova, nec priores
impiae tectum dominae relinquunt,
    saepe minati.

te suis matres metuunt iuvencis,
te senes parci miseraeque, nuper
virgines, nuptae, tua ne retardet
    aura maritos.

II.8

Were even a single penalty incurred, Barina, for the sum
of all your violated vows, or were you one tooth uglier,
one nail more broken, for the now-enormous volume
of your broken word,

I might be able to believe you. Instead, no sooner have you staked
your faithless life on something, than you turn to dazzle—
beauty blazes up in you, and catches off-guard every naked
eye: you traffic hazard!

You swear on your mother's grave, for sakes alive;
you perjure the wordless stars, and their whole sky; you take
the names of the gods in vain (who feel no coldness visited on men)
—and still you thrive.

Venus herself must find it droll, and all her smiling retinue
of artless nymphs condone, and even heartless
Cupid too—forever blading his arrowheads
on bloody stone.

That's not to mention scores of youngsters born and bred
for you, your new love-slaves; and all the venerable
hearts once set on you, who never could escape your stable,
though they threaten to;

and mothers afraid their well-made sons are doomed, and tight
old stiffs their money; and even the hapless newlywed, worried awake
so late—(so soon!)—lest a whiff of your musk in the night waylay
the swaying groom.

Heather McHugh

Non semper imbres nubibus hispidos
manant in agros aut mare Caspium
   vexant inaequales procellae
      usque nec Armeniis in oris,

amice Valgi, stat glacies iners
menses per omnes, aut Aquilonibus
   querqueta Gargani laborant
      et foliis viduantur orni:

tu semper urges flebilibus modis
Mysten ademptum, nec tibi Vespero
   surgente decedunt amores
      nec rapidum fugiente solem.

at non ter aevo functus amabilem
ploravit omnes Antilochum senex
   annos, nec impubem parentes
      Troilon aut Phrygiae sorores

flevere semper. desine mollium
tandem querellarum, et potius nova
   cantemus Augusti tropaea
      Caesaris, et rigidum Niphaten

Medumque flumen gentibus additum
victis minores volvere vertices,
   intraque praescriptum Gelonos
      exiguis equitare campis.

II.9

Clouds do not send their rain down endlessly
On the rough-whiskered fields, nor do
Dogged gales work up the Caspian Sea
All year, nor in Armenia, dear friend,

Do glaciers remain inert month after month,
Nor do those rough oak-forested headlands
Poking out into the Adriatic suffer squalls that
Pull leaves continually away from their branches.

But you now weepily carry on about
The initiate in love you lost; your moans do
Not sink even when the Western Star rises,
Nor when the Morning Star hurries away at dawn.

And yet that old man Nestor, who had lived three
Lives, did not mourn his son forever;
When they lost Troilus the lovable, his
Phrygian sisters and parents did not go on

And on. So it's good to check your endless
Lamentations; instead, let's take note of the gains
That our Caesar, called the Augustus, has
Made in the world—some Turkish peaks

Are lower now, the Euphrates waters are
A bit more constrained, the Medes are part
Of the Empire these days, and the Scythians riding
Over the steppes are, in fact, no longer nomads.

Robert Bly

II.10

Rectius vives, Licini, neque altum
semper urgendo neque, dum procellas
cautus horrescis, nimium premendo
    litus iniquum.

auream quisquis mediocritatem
diligit, tutus caret obsoleti
sordibus tecti, caret invidenda
    sobrius aula.

saepius ventis agitatur ingens
pinus et celsae graviore casu
decidunt turres feriuntque summos
    fulgura montis.

sperat infestis, metuit secundis
alteram sortem bene praeparatum
pectus. informes hiemes reducit
    Iuppiter; idem

summovet. non, si male nunc, et olim
sic erit: quondam cithara tacentem
suscitat Musam neque semper arcum
    tendit Apollo.

rebus angustis animosus atque
fortis appare: sapienter idem
contrahes vento nimium secundo
    turgida vela.

II.10

Neither should one, Licinius, beat forever
For the open sea, nor from a fear of gales
Become too cautious, and too closely hug
    The jagged shore.

A man who cherishes the golden mean
Has too much sense to live in a squalid house,
Yet sensibly eschews the sort of mansion
    That asks for envy.

It is the tall pine that the wind more cruelly
Buffets, the high tower that falls with the heavier
Crash; and it is the very crest of the mountain
    Where lightning strikes.

A heart that is prepared for shifts of fortune
Hopes in adversity, and in happy times
Is wary. Jupiter brings afflicting winter,
    And the same god

Takes it away. Today's ill luck will someday
Change for the better: sometimes Apollo wakens
The slumbering lyre to song, nor is he always
    Bending the bow.

In every hardship show yourself to be
Both brave and bold; yet when you run before
Too strong a favoring breeze, wisely take in
    Your swelling sails.

                    Richard Wilbur

II.11

Quid bellicosus Cantaber et Scythes,
Hirpine Quincti, cogitet Hadria
   divisus obiecto, remittas
      quaerere, nec trepides in usum

poscentis aevi pauca: fugit retro
levis iuventas et decor, arida
   pellente lascivos amores
      canitie facilemque somnum.

non semper idem floribus est honor
vernis, neque uno luna rubens nitet
   voltu: quid aeternis minorem
      consiliis animum fatigas?

cur non sub alta vel platano vel hac
pinu iacentes sic temere et rosa
   canos odorati capillos,
      dum licet, Assyriaque nardo

potamus uncti? dissipat Euhius
curas edaces. quis puer ocius
   restinguet ardentis Falerni
      pocula praetereunte lympha?

quis devium scortum eliciet domo
Lyden? eburna, dic age, cum lyra
   maturet, in comptum Lacaenae
      more comas religata nodum!

II.11

Don't worry about it, Quinctius. Don't fret.
Whatever they plan, the Cantabrians and the Scythians—
Divided from us by the Adriatic sea—
    Signifies almost nothing. Life is short,

    And asks little of us. How soon the bright
Days of our youth and beauty end, and age
Puts paid to love and ease and the small gift
    Of going out like a light.

    The wildflowers of spring will not inherit
The earth forever nor the moon shine like this.
Why do you weary yourself? Why do you worry
    The infinite question with your finite spirit?

    Why not drink this wine under the airy
Plane trees and pines while we can, our silver hair
Reddened with rose petals and fragrant with
    The sweet oils and balsam of Syria?

    For the god of wine is the enemy of care.
And which slave-boy will bring us water now
From a fast stream to cool down and temper
    Our bowls of Falernian fire?

    And as for Lyde, who is going to persuade her,
Shy as she is, to leave home and join us? Tell her to hurry.
Tell her to come, dressed Laconian-style, with
    Her ivory lyre and her hair neatly tied.

Eavan Boland

II.12

Nolis longa ferae bella Numantiae
nec durum Hannibalem nec Siculum mare
Poeno purpureum sanguine mollibus
    aptari citharae modis,

nec saevos Lapithas et nimium mero
Hylaeum domitosque Herculea manu
telluris iuvenes, unde periculum
    fulgens contremuit domus

Saturni veteris: tuque pedestribus
dices historiis proelia Caesaris,
Maecenas, melius ductaque per vias
    regum colla minacium.

me dulces dominae Musa Licymniae
cantus, me voluit dicere lucidum
fulgentes oculos et bene mutuis
    fidum pectus amoribus;

quam nec ferre pedem dedecuit choris
nec certare ioco nec dare bracchia
ludentem nitidis virginibus sacro
    Dianae celebris die.

num tu quae tenuit dives Achaemenes
aut pinguis Phrygiae Mygdonias opes
permutare velis crine Licymniae,
    plenas aut Arabum domos,

cum flagrantia detorquet ad oscula
cervicem, aut facili saevitia negat,
quae poscente magis gaudeat eripi,
    interdum rapere occupat?

132

II. 12

Spare me the Roman wars, and those
Who battled on in myth, when prose
Extends to suit these topics better
Than odes in their mellifluous meter.

Maecenas, think on this awhile:
Strong themes are suited to your style,
Like dragging tyrants by their necks,
While my sweet Muse would sing of sex,

Of my fair lady, Licymnia,
Who fondly hopes her heart will be a
Faithful devotee of mine
With eyes as shimmering as wine.

See how she glories at the chance
To show her prowess in the dance.
Though lightly clad, she's not the least
Shy of display at Diana's feast.

Tell me, Maecenas, wouldn't you
Abjure all wealth, and treasure too
If Licymnia would choose to spare
One strand of her luxuriant hair?

Even if this flirtatious miss
Denies you the favor of one kiss
To disconcert you, makes you feel it,
She won't accept your kiss; she'll steal it!

Carolyn Kizer

Ille et nefasto te posuit die,
quicumque primum, et sacrilega manu
   produxit, arbos, in nepotum
      perniciem opprobriumque pagi.

illum et parentis crediderim sui
fregisse cervicem et penetralia
   sparsisse nocturno cruore
      hospitis; ille venena Colcha

et quicquid usquam concipitur nefas
tractavit, agro qui statuit meo
   te, triste lignum, te caducum
      in domini caput immerentis.

quid quisque vitet, numquam homini satis
cautum est in horas: navita Bosphorum
   Poenus perhorrescit neque ultra
      caeca timet aliunde fata;

miles sagittas et celerem fugam
Parthi, cartenas Parthus et Italum
   robur; sed improvisa leti
      vis rapuit rapietque gentes.

quam paene furvae regna Proserpinae
et iudicantem vidimus Aeacum
   sedesque discriptas piorum et
      Aeoliis fidibus querentem

Sappho puellis de popularibus
et te sonantem plenius aureo,
   Alcaee, plectro dura navis,
      dura fugae mala, dura belli.

He planted you on a malignant day, whoever
first tamped your roots down, tree; with a cursed hand
   he raised you to blight the future
      and shame the countryside.

He throttled his own father, I'd believe,
and spattered his fireplace with a guest's blood at night;
   he deals in Colchian poisons
      and any crime cooked up

in the mind of man, the one who established you
in my field, rotten, corrupted tree, to fall
   all of a sudden on the head
      of your innocent master.

From one hour to the next, man never knows
how to sidestep danger: the Punic sailor
   shudders at the Bosphorus but hardly
      thinks of the threats beyond;

the soldier dreads the Parthian's arrows and swift
retreat, the Parthian fears Italy's chains and force;
   but fate, in violence, by surprise, has seized,
      and will seize, every people on earth.

I came within a breath of seeing dark Proserpina's realm
and Aeacus sitting in judgment, and the halls
   set aside for the just; I almost saw
      Sappho with her Aeolian lyre

sobbing for the girls of Lesbos; and you, Alcaeus, playing
more fully as you pluck the strings with your golden pick,
   of sorrows at sea, sorrows endured
      in exile, sorrows of war.

utrumque sacro digna silentio
mirantur umbrae dicere; sed magis
   pugnas et exactos tyrannos
      densum umeris bibit aure volgus.

quid mirum, ubi illis carminibus stupens
demittit atras belua centiceps
   auris, et intorti capillis
      Eumenidum recreantur angues?

quin et Prometheus et Pelopis parens
dulci laborum decipitur sono,
   nec curat Orion leones
      aut timidos agitare lyncas.

The shades listen, marveling, as both
sing words compelling a sacred hush; but most,
   packed shoulder to shoulder, the crowd drinks in
     stories of war, of banished tyrants.

No wonder the hundred-headed monster, drugged
by such songs, droops his black ears, and the snakes
   twined in the Furies' hair
     pause in their writhing.

Even Prometheus and Tantalus are seduced
from their torments by the honeyed sound,
   and Orion leaves off chasing
     lions and cautious lynxes.

                  Rosanna Warren

II.14

Eheu fugaces, Postume, Postume,
labuntur anni, nec pietas moram
   rugis et instanti senectae
     adferet indomitaeque morti;

non, si trecenis, quotquot eunt dies,
amice, places inlacrimabilem
   Plutona tauris, qui ter amplum
     Geryonen Tityonque tristi

compescit unda, scilicet omnibus,
quicumque terrae munere vescimur,
   enaviganda, sive reges
     sive iopes erimus coloni.

frustra cruento Marte carebimus
fractisque rauci fluctibus Hadriae,
   frustra per autumnos nocentem
     corporibus metuemus Austrum:

visendus ater flumine languido
Cocytos errans et Danai genus
   infame damnatusque longi
     Sisyphus Aeolides laboris.

linquenda tellus et domus et placens
uxor, neque harum, quas colis, arborum
   te praeter invasas cupressos
     ulla brevem dominum sequetur.

absumet heres Caecuba dignior
servata centum clavibus et mero
   tinguet pavimentum superbo
     pontificum potiore cenis.

II.14

The fleeing years, Postumus, Postumus, how they
go gliding swiftly by, nor may our devotion
   delay the wrinkles, halt the march of
      age that approaches, of Death unconquered.

Not even if with three hundred oxen daily
you tried to placate pitiless Pluto who in
   confinement still keeps Tityos, and
      three-bodied Geryon, by the gloom of

the waves across which all of us must get ferried,
who live on all the gifts of the land, and whether
   or not they be the princes of the
      realm, or the poorest of simple farmhands.

No use escaping Mars and his cruelty, nor
the hoarsely breaking waves of the Adriatic,
   no use to fear throughout the autumn
      winds from the south that will harm our bodies:

We have to watch meandering, black Cocytus
and Danaus' infamous bunch of daughters.
   We have to gaze on Aeolus' offspring
      Sisyphus, doomed to his stretch of labor.

We have to leave the land and our home and pleasing
wife, nor will any one of these trees you've tended
   be following their all too short-lived
      master, except for the hateful cypress.

An heir more worthy soon will consume your vintage
Caecuban—locked up now by a hundred keys—and
   stain the paved floor with a grander
      wine than is drunk at the feasts of Pontiffs.

John Hollander

II.15

Iam pauca aratro iugera regiae
moles relinquent, undique latius
    extenta visentur Lucrino
        stagna lacu, platanusque caelebs

evincet ulmos; tum violaria et
myrtus et omnis copia narium
    spargent olivetis odorem
        fertilibus domino priori.

tum spissa ramis laurea fervidos
excludet ictus. non ita Romuli
    praescriptum et intonsi Catonis
        auspiciis veterumque norma.

privatus illis census erat brevis,
commune magnum: nulla decempedis
    metata privatis opacam
        porticus excipiebat Arcton,

nec fortuitum spernere caespitem
leges sinebant, oppida publico
    sumptu iubentes et deorum
        templa novo decorare saxo.

Before long, the estates of the rich
and their fish ponds bigger than a lake
will cover what few acres
are still left for the plow.

Plane trees will drive out the vine-loving elms.
Myrtle woods and beds of violets
and other sweet-scented blooms
will make fragrant the olive grove

that kept the farmer prosperous.
Thick-branched laurels will protect
against sunstroke. That's not how
things were here in the old days:

Romulus and curly-bearded Cato
would have despised our ways.
Their private holdings were modest,
the communal property large.

No private citizen could afford
to build a vast, north-facing portico
just to trap its cool shade.
Houses had thatch roofs then

Yet nobody was ashamed.
The law obliged them to pretty up
their towns and their temples
with freshly quarried marble.

Charles Simic

II.16

Otium divos rogat in patenti
prensus Aegaeo, simul atra nubes
condidit lunam neque certa fulgent
    sidera nautis;

otium bello furiosa Thrace,
otium Medi pharetra decori,
Grosphe, non gemmis neque purpura ve-
    nale neque auro.

non enim gazae neque consularis
summovet lictor miseros tumultus
mentis et curas laqueata circum
    tecta volantes.

vivitur parvo bene, cui paternum
splendet in mensa tenui salinum
nec leves somnos timor aut cupido
    sordidus aufert.

quid brevi fortes iaculamur aevo
multa? quid terras alio calentes
sole mutamus? patriae quis exsul
    se quoque fugit?

scandit aeratas vitiosa naves
cura nec turmas equitum relinquit,
ocior cervis et agente nimbos
    ocior Euro.

laetus in praesens animus quod ultra est
oderit curare et amara lento
temperet risu. nihil est ab omni
    parte beatum.

II.16

When storm clouds closing in darken the sea
and cover the moon and hide the stars that might
have guided him across rough waters, the sailor
    prays for peace;

the battle-weary Thracians pray for peace,
the Parthians with their fancy daggers
pray for peace, but peace cannot be bought
    with purple, gold or gems;

and peace cannot be won with rank or money,
neither one can ease the soul's distress,
the worries and the nagging fears that flit
    about in paneled rooms.

A man can please himself with little, a salt dish
handed down for generations can gleam upon
his table, and his sleep will not be ruined by
    the sordidness of greed.

So why do we waste our time chasing down
possessions? Why do we leave home and head south
to a foreign land, a foreign sun? Who really
    can escape himself?

Trouble leaps aboard the rich man's brigantine,
outruns the fastest horse, the nimblest deer,
is swifter than Eurus, the bad-weather wind
    responsible for storms.

We should be happy in the here and now
and unconcerned with what the future holds;
we should blunt the edge of sorrow with a smile.
    There is no perfect joy.

abstulit clarum cita mors Achillem,
longa Tithonum minuit senectus;
et mihi forsan, tibi quod negarit,
    porriget hora.

te greges centum Siculaeque circum
mugiunt vaccae, tibi tollit hinnitum
apta quadrigis equa, te bis Afro
    murice tinctae

vestiunt lanae; mihi parva rura et
spiritum Graiae tenuem Camenae
Parca non mendax dedit et malignum
    spernere vulgus.

Achilles met with death when he was young,
Tithonus lived on to be the shadow of
his former self; and fate might give to me
    what it withholds from you.

Your fields are filled with lowing herds of prime
Sicilian cattle, and from your stable you
can hear the whinnies of your racing mare;
    the clothes you have are made

of wool twice-dyed in African purple, whereas
it is my lot to have a smallish house,
a gift for turning Greek verse into Latin,
    and scorn for the envious.

                    Mark Strand

II.17

Cur me querellis exanimas tuis?
nec dis amicum est nec mihi te prius
    obire, Maecenas, mearum
        grande decus columenque rerum.

a, te meae si partem animae rapit
maturior vis, quid moror altera,
    nec carus aeque nec superstes
        integer? ille dies utramque

ducet ruinam. non ego perfidum
dixi sacramentum: ibimus, ibimus,
    utcumque praecedes, supremum
        carpere iter comites parati.

me nec Chimaerae spiritus igneae
nec, si resurgat, centimanus Gyas
    divellet umquam: sic potenti
        Iustitiae placitumque Parcis.

seu Libra seu me Scorpios adspicit
formidolosus pars violentior
    natalis horae seu tyrannus
        Hesperiae Capricornus undae,

utrumque nostrum incredibili modo
consentit astrum. te Iovis impio
    tutela Saturno refulgens
        eripuit volucrisque Fati

tardavit alas, cum populus frequens
laetum theatris ter crepuit sonum;
    me truncus inlapsus cerebro
        sustulerat, nisi Faunus ictum

dextra levasset, Mercurialium
custos virorum. reddere victimas
    aedemque votivam memento;
        nos humilem feriemus agnam.

II.17

Why torture me to death with your complaints?
Neither the gods nor I would have me fall
    Before you fall yourself, Maecenas,
        Roof-tree of my life.

If some precocious bolt should shatter you,
Why, how could I, whom you have sheltered, your
    Alter ego, survive? Since halves,
        We have to go at once.

I took my vow. Whenever you must go,
Then go must I. I, too. We two—together,
    Closer than twins—will take our journey's
        Final step together.

The Fates concur with Justice's verdict:
No flame-throwing Chimera will ever part
    Us now, no hundred-handed Gyges
        Rip my limbs from yours.

Regardless whether Libra, or violent
Scorpio, or lambent Capricorn
    Presided at my birth, we are
        Ourselves a double star.

Famously, Jove saved you from Saturn's sentence.
He fought off the Death, falling on sudden wings
    Towards you, whose dramatic rescue
        Brought the people to

Their feet to call you back for three encores.
And as for me, that falling tree was de-
    flected by Faunus, deputy
        Of Mercury, patron

Of thieves and poets. Remember your own vow:
Build the proper altar, and sacrifice
    The promised hecatomb. Me,
        I'll offer up my lamb.

Stephen Yenser

II.18

Non ebur neque aureum
    mea renidet in domo lacunar,
non trabes Hymettiae
    premunt columnas ultima recisas

Africa, neque Attali
    ignotus heres regiam occupavi,
nec Laconicas mihi
    trahunt honestae purpuras clientae.

at fides et ingeni
    benigna vena est, pauperemque dives
me petit: nihil supra
    deos lacesso nec potentem amicum

largiora flagito,
    satis beatus unicis Sabinis.
truditur dies die,
    novaeque pergunt interire lunae.

tu secanda marmora
    locas sub ipsum funus et sepulcri
immemor struis domos,
    marisque Bais obstrepentis urges

summovere litora,
    parum locuples continente ripa.
quid quod usque proximos
    revellis agri terminos et ultra

limites clientium
    salis avarus? pellitur paternos
in sinu ferens deos
    et uxor et vir sordidosque natos.

II. 18

You'll find no gold or ivory panels
    gleaming in my house,
no beams of Hymettian marble
    bearing down on pillars
shipped all the way from Africa,
    nor have I—one of the mock heirs of Attalus—
suddenly become the owner of a mansion,
    nor do fashionable women come swiveling
their Laconian-purple robes my way.
    And yet, though poor, I'm courted
by rich men because I'm a loyal
    amiable genius. I ask nothing more
of the gods. I long for nothing
    from my friends in power
but what I already have: my dear
    Sabine farm. Each day dogs the heels
of another day, and new moons return
    and hurry again to darkness.
But you, on the edge of the grave,
    are signing even more agreements
for the cutting and polishing of marble slabs
    (why don't they remind you
of your tomb?) and are building a palace
    on the loud, frothy seacoast
of Baiae, the mainland shore not quite
    exclusive enough for you. You're tearing down
the boundaries of your estate, encroaching
    on your neighboring tenants
and driving them off with ragged children
    and household gods in their arms.
And yet the really up-to-date space
    every wealthy lord is destined to occupy

nulla certior tamen
    rapacis Orci fine destinata
aula divitem manet
    erum. quid ultra tendis? aequa tellus

pauperi recluditur
    regumque pueris, nec satelles Orci
callidum Promethea
    revexit auro captus. hic superbum

Tantalum atque Tantali
    genus coercet, hic levare functum
pauperem laboribus
    vocatus atque non vocatus audit.

belongs to ravenous Death. Why work so hard
    for yours? For all of us, for the poor
as well as the sons of princes, the same earth
    lies open. Not even crafty Prometheus
could manage to bribe that Ferryman
    with gold. Death holds fast
both Tantalus and the sons of Tantalus
    whether they like it or not
and listens only to the poor man
    and sets him free when his work is done.

David Wagoner

II.19

Bacchum in remotis carmina rupibus
vidi docentem—credite posteri—
    Nymphasque discentes et auris
        capripedum Satyrorum acutas.

euhoe, recenti mens trepidat metu,
plenoque Bacchi pectore turbidum
    laetatur. euhoe, parce, Liber,
        parce, gravi metuende thyrso.

fas pervicaces est mihi Thyiadas
vinique fontem lactis et uberes
    cantare rivos atque truncis
        lapsa cavis iterare mella;

fas et beatae coniugis additum
stellis honorem tectaque Penthei
    disiecta non leni ruina
        Thracis et exitium Lycurgi.

tu flectis amnes, tu mare barbarum,
tu separatis uvidus in iugis
    nodo coerces viperino
        Bistonidum sine fraude crines.

tu, cum parentis regna per arduum
cohors Gigantum scanderet impia,
    Rhoetum retorsisti leonis
        unguibus horribilique mala;

quamquam choreis aptior et iocis
ludoque dictus non sat idoneus
    pugnae ferebaris; sed idem
        pacis eras mediusque belli.

te vidit insons Cerberus aureo
cornu decorum, leniter atterens
    caudam, et recedentis trilingui
        ore pedes tetigitque crura.

Bacchus himself. Believe me, children, I
found Bacchus himself right there, teaching
   songs to the nymphs and satyrs.
      You've heard of their goatfeet?

Their pointed ears? I'm shaking at the thought
of it. So spare me, Bacchus. Liber,
   with your dreadful rod. I'm only
      following orders here, you've made

me do it, made me praise those women wild
with love of you, those happy fonts of milk
   and wine, those hollows thick
      with honey. Made me chant the story of

your twice-blessed bride, her crown installed
among the stars, and Pentheus, his house dispersed
   in ruins, and Lycurgus dead in Thrace.
      Bad end to non-believers.

You—shall I go on?—you part the seas, you
change the course of rivers. Flushed with wine,
   among the far-flung hills, you bind
      the writhing hair of girls with writhing knots

of snakes. And once, when a band of overgrown
usurpers tried to mount your father's throne,
   you fought them like a lion tooth
      and claw. I've heard it said

your talent is for games, not war. But I say
your heroics take the bay on every
   playing field, in battle and in mirth
      alike. How else construe the welcome

you received in Hell? When Cerberus beheld your
golden horn he lost all taste for harm.
   He rubbed against you with his tail.
      He licked your feet with his three tongues.

                              Linda Gregerson

Non usitata nec tenui ferar
pinna biformis per liquidum aethera
   vates, neque in terris morabor
     longius invidiaque maior

urbes relinquam. non ego, pauperum
sanguis parentum, non ego, quem vocas,
   dilecte Maecenas, obibo
     nec Stygia cohibebor unda.

iam iam residunt cruribus asperae
pelles, et album mutor in alitem
   superne, nascunturque leves
     per digitos umerosque plumae.

iam Daedaleo notior Icaro
visam gementis litora Bosphori
   Syrtesque Gaetulas canorus
     ales Hyperboreosque campos.

me Colchus et, qui dissimulat metum
Marsae cohortis, Dacus et ultimi
   noscent Geloni, me peritus
     discet Hiber Rhodanique potor.

absint inani funere neniae
luctusque turpes et querimoniae;
   compesce clamorem ac sepulcri
     mitte supervacuos honores.

II.20

It won't be any feeble,
Ordinary wings
I'll rise on, through liquid aether—

I, still a poet, not earthbound,
Triumphing over envy
And leaving all human cities far behind.

Not I, son of poor parents,
Not I, who came to know
Your voice, dear friend Maecenas—

Not I shall merely perish
Nor wander by the Styx.
Look—even now the skin around my ankles

Has been transformed, I
Am changing into a swan,
The feathers sprouting from my arms

And shoulders are white as snow,
My sleek plumage. A singing bird
Bolder than Icarus the son of Daedalus,

I will fly high above the shores
Where the Bosphorus moans. I'll scan
Syrtes and the Hyperborean plains.

They'll know me in Colchia,
The Hungarians will know me, even
Remote tribes who claim they don't fear Rome

Will come to know me, too.
They'll study my poems in Spain
To become learned, and also in Germany—

Omit my funeral dirges,
Don't grieve at all, spare me
The unnecessary tribute of a tomb.

Robert Pinsky

LIBER | BOOK III

III.1

Odi profanum vulgus et arceo;
favete linguis. carmina non prius
   audita Musarum sacerdos
      virginibus puerisque canto.

regum timendorum in proprios greges,
reges in ipsos imperium est Iovis,
   clari Giganteo triumpho,
      cuncta supercilio moventis.

est ut viro vir latius ordinet
arbusta sulcis, hic generosior
   descendat in Campum petitor,
      moribus hic meliorque fama

contendat, illi turba clientium
sit maior; aequa lege Necessitas
   sortitur insignes et imos:
      omne capax movet urna nomen.

destrictus ensis cui super impia
cervice pendet, non Siculae dapes
   dulcem elaborabunt saporem,
      non avium citharaeque cantus

somnum reducent. somnus agrestium
lenis virorum non humiles domos
   fastidit umbrosamque ripam,
      non zephyris agitata Tempe.

desiderantem quod satis est neque
tumultuosum sollicitat mare
   nec saevus Arcturi cadentis
      impetus aut orientis Haedi,

III. 1

I hate and keep away the unholy crowd.
Hush, then! for in the silence of reverence
   I sing songs never heard before, as
      Priest of the Muse, for girls and boys now.

Kings rule, intimidating, their flock; the kings
are governed in their turn by Jove, all glorious
   in conquering the Giants, he who,
      twitching his eyebrow, controls the cosmos.

One man, no doubt, has planted his vines in rows
more widely spaced apart than another's; one
   will come down to the Field of Mars, a
      candidate, nobler by birth, another

of greater fame and character, and a third
with larger mobs of followers, and yet Fate
   treats High and Low impartially: the
      ballot urn, roomy, keeps all names shuffled.

For him above whose impious head there hangs
the naked sword, Sicilian feasts can shape
   no savory delights, nor any
      music of birds nor of lyres can send him

again to sleep; yet sleep untroubled will not
disdain the humblest farmer's abode, nor bank
   of shaded stream, nor, ruffled by the
      gentlest of zephyrs, the Vale of Tempe.

But he who longs for no more than what he needs
is never put upon by tumultuous seas
   nor by the savage battering of
      setting Arcturus or Haedus rising,

non verberatae grandine vineae
fundusque mendax, arbore nunc aquas
   culpante, nunc torrentia agros
      sidera, nunc hiemes iniquas.

contracta pisces aequora sentiunt
iactis in altum molibus: huc frequens
   caementa demittit redemptor
      cum famulis dominusque terrae

fastidiosus. sed Timor et Minae
scandunt eodem quo dominus, neque
   decedit aerata triremi et
      post equitem sedet atra Cura.

quodsi dolentem nec Phrygius lapis
nec purpurarum sidere clarior
   delenit usus nec Falerna
      vitis Achaemeniumque costum,

cur invidendis postibus et novo
sublime ritu moliar atrium?
   cur valle permutem Sabina
      divitias operosiores?

nor by his vineyards being whipped down with hail
nor by his farm's deceitfulness, olive trees
   now blaming all the rain, now Dog Star,
      scorching the fields, now uneven winters.

The fish can sense the narrowing of their streams
by rocky dams set deep, where the builder with
   his gang of slaves cast rubble for the
      owner disdaining to merely build on

the ground. But Fears and Menaces climb up there
around an owner, nor will black Worry quit
   his bronze-bedoodled yacht, and always,
      when he goes riding, sits right behind him.

And still, if neither Phrygian marble, robes
of purple far more glittering than the stars,
   can ease my anguish now, nor Persian
      scent, nor yet the Falernian vintage,

why should I work to pile up a lofty hall
with columns to be envied—the newest style;
   why should I change my Sabine vale for
      all of the heavier load of riches?

John Hollander

III.2

Angustam amice pauperiem pati
robustus acri militia puer
   condiscat et Parthos feroces
      vexet eques metuendus hasta,

vitamque sub divo et trepidis agat
in rebus. illum ex moenibus hosticis
   matrona bellantis tyranni
      prospiciens et adulta virgo

suspiret: "eheu, ne rudis agminum
sponsus lacessat regius asperum
   tactu leonem, quem cruenta
      per medias rapit ira caedes."

dulce et decorum est pro patria mori.
mors et fugacem persequitur virum,
   nec parcit imbellis iuventae
      poplitibus timidove tergo.

Virtus, repulsae nescia sordidae,
intaminatis fulget honoribus,
   nec sumit aut ponit secures
      arbitrio popularis aurae.

Virtus, recludens immeritis mori
caelum, negata temptat iter via,
   coetusque vulgares et udam
      spernit humum fugiente pinna.

est et fideli tuta silentio
merces: vetabo, qui Cereris sacrum
   volgarit arcanae, sub isdem
      sit trabibus fragilemque mecum

solvat phaselon; saepe Diespiter
neglectus incesto addidit integrum,
   raro antecedentem scelestum
      deseruit pede Poena claudo.

III.2

Let youth, toughened by a soldier's training,
Learn to bear hardship gladly,
And to harry the fierce Parthians
With a spear from the back of a horse,

And to live boldly under an open sky,
So that, seeing him from an enemy rampart,
Some warring king's wife, looking on,
Will turn to the young woman beside her,

Sighing: Oh, let's hope our young prince
Doesn't stir up that rough-skinned lion
Whom a cruel rage for blood drives
Straight to the middle of the slaughter.

Honorable and sweet to die for one's country,
Since death doesn't spare the deserter either
Nor the boy without a warrior's instinct
Who goes down with his back and tendons slashed.

Real worth isn't determined in elections;
Of itself it shines out undefiled.
It neither picks up a public office
Nor puts it down at the public's whim.

Worth, opening heaven to those death
Cannot claim, makes its journey on a path
Not known to the vulgar crowd and flees
The damp earth on feathered wings.

Knowing when to be silent has also its reward.
I wouldn't sit under the same roofbeams
Or set sail in the same boat with someone
Who divulged the secret rites of Ceres.

Often enough Jupiter has been known
To punish the innocent along with the guilty,
And Vengeance rarely misses the wicked it means,
With its limping gait, to track down.

Robert Hass

III.3

Iustum et tenacem propositi virum
non civium ardor prava iubentium,
   non vultus instantis tyranni
      mente quatit solida neque Auster,

dux inquieti turbidus Hadriae,
nec fulminantis magna manus Iovis;
   si fractus inlabatur orbis,
      impavidum ferient ruinae.

hac arte Pollux et vagus Hercules
enisus arces attigit igneas,
   quos inter Augustus recumbens
      purpureo bibet ore nectar.

hac te merentem, Bacche pater, tuae
vexere tigres, indocili iugum
   collo trahentes; hac Quirinus
      Martis equis Acheronta fugit,

gratum elocuta consiliantibus
Iunone divis: "Ilion, Ilion
   fatalis incestusque iudex
      et mulier peregrina vertit

in pulverem, ex quo destituit deos
mercede pacta Laomedon, mihi
   castaeque damnatum Minervae
      cum populo et duce fraudulento.

III.3

The man who is just, and holds
fixed to his purpose—nothing
shakes him from his resolve:

not the fervor of citizens eager
for depravities, not the face of
some tyrant on the rise, not

the south wind, unruly master
of the ever-restive Adriatic, not even
the mighty hand of thundering Jove.

If the world itself should fall
asunder, the ruins strike down
a man who knows no fear. It's

this way that Pollux and wandering
Hercules strove for and reached
the starlit citadels, even as

Augustus, at ease among them,
will drink nectar, too, his mouth
red with it. In the same way,

father Bacchus, your tigers wearing
the yoke on their untamed necks,
bore you to the heaven you deserved.

So too, Quirinus, on the horses of
Mars, escaped Acheron, when Juno
pleased the assembled gods by saying:

"A fateful, debauched judge
and a foreign woman turn Troy
into the dust, now—Troy, its

people, its treacherous leader,
all deeded to me and to chaste
Minerva when Laomedon cheated

iam nec Lacaenae splendet adulterae
famosus hospes nec Priami domus
   periura pugnaces Achivos
      Hectoreis opibus refringit,

nostrisque ductum seditionibus
bellum resedit. protinus et graves
   iras et invisum nepotem,
      Troica quem peperit sacerdos,

Marti redonabo; illum ego lucidas
inire sedes, ducere nectaris
   sucos et adscribi quietis
      ordinibus patiar deorum.

dum longus inter saeviat Ilion
Romamque pontus, qualibet exsules
   in parte regnanto beati;
      dum Priami Paridisque busto

insultet armentum et catulos ferae
celent inultae, stet Capitolium
   fulgens triumphatisque possit
      Roma ferox dare iura Medis.

horrenda late nomen in ultimas
extendat oras, qua medius liquor
   secernit Europen ab Afro,
      qua tumidus rigat arva Nilus,

the gods of their settled price.
No longer does the infamous
guest and stranger shine for

the Spartan adulteress, nor
does the perjured house of Priam
hold at bay by Hector's prowess

the warring Greeks, and a war
drawn out by our own feuding
now is ended, my anger too; I

return my hated grandson—
child of the Trojan priestess—
to Mars, and let him enter our

bright kingdom, drink nectar,
be counted among the peaceful
ranks of the gods.

So long as there rages between
Troy and Rome a wide sea,
let the exiles rule somewhere

happily. So long as cattle
tread upon the tomb of Priam
and Paris, and wild beasts

unpunished hide their young there,
let the gleaming Capitol stand,
let fierce Rome hold sway

over the conquered Medes. Held
everywhere in awe, let her spread
her name to the farthest shores,

where the sea divides Europe
from Africa, where the swollen
Nile, flooding the fields, is more

aurum inrepertum et sic melius situm,
cum terra celat, spernere fortior
   quam cogere humanos in usus
      omne sacrum rapiente dextra.

quicumque mundo terminus obstitit,
hunc tangat armis, visere gestiens,
   qua parte debacchentur ignes,
      qua nebulae pluviique rores.

sed bellicosis fata Quiritibus
hac lege dico, ne nimium pii
   rebusque fidentes avitae
      tecta velint reparare Troiae.

Troiae renascens alite lugubri
fortuna tristi clade iterabitur
   ducente victrices catervas
      coniuge me Iovis et sorore.

ter si resurgat murus aëneus
auctore Phoebo, ter pereat meis
   excisus Argivis, ter uxor
      capta virum puerosque ploret."

non hoc iocosae conveniet lyrae:
quo, Musa, tendis? desine pervicax
   referre sermones deorum et
      magna modis tenuare parvis.

able to spurn undiscovered gold
(and thus better placed, while
the earth hides it) than the hand

that plunders everything sacred
can gather it for human uses.
Whatever limits there are to the world,

let her reach it with her armies,
eager to see to where fiery heat
rages—where mists, where rains.

But I announce to the warlike
Quirites their fate on this condition:
that they not, being overly dutiful,

upright, and too confident in their
resources, wish to restore the roofs
of ancestral Troy. If Troy's fortune

rises again, ill-omened it will do so,
and her utter disaster, too, will be
repeated—I myself, Jove's wife and

sister, shall lead the conquering forces.
If the bronze wall should rise
three times with the aid of Phoebus,

three times my Argives will destroy it,
three times the captured wife will
mourn her sons and husband."

—This is no subject for the playful
lyre: my Muse, where are you off to?
Enough of your willful reports

about the gods' assemblies,
your meter isn't up to it. Stop
making great matters less so.

Carl Phillips

III.4

Descende caelo et dic age tibia
regina longum Calliope melos,
   seu voce nunc mavis acuta
      seu fidibus citharaque Phoebi.

auditis, an me ludit amabilis
insania? audire et videor pios
   errare per lucos, amoenae
      quos et aquae subeunt et aurae.

me fabulosae Volture in avio
nutricis extra limen Apuliae
   ludo fatigatumque somno
      fronde nova puerum palumbes

texere, mirum quod foret omnibus,
quicumque celsae nidum Acherontiae
   saltusque Bantinos et arvum
      pingue tenent humilis Forenti,

ut tuto ab atris corpore viperis
dormirem et ursis, ut premerer sacra
   lauroque conlataque myrto,
      non sine dis animosus infans.

vester, Camenae, vester in arduos
tollor Sabinos, seu mihi frigidum
   Praeneste seu Tibur supinum
      seu liquidae placuere Baiae.

vestris amicum fontibus et choris
non me Phillippis versa acies retro,
   devota non extinxit arbor,
      nec Sicula Palinurus unda.

III.4

Descend from heaven, divine Calliope,
And play upon your flute a long slow song
   Or, accompanied by Apollo's lyre,
      Sing in your own clear voice.

Can you hear her? Or does some sweet madness
Mock me? I'd swear I hear her, and am wandering
   Through the hallowed grove, its soothing streams
      And breezes mingling.

Once, as a boy, straying too far from my nurse
On the slopes of wild Mount Vultur, I tired
   Of my games and fell asleep. As in the fable,
      Wood-doves covered me

With fresh-fallen leaves, a wonder to those who dwell
Nestled in high Acherontia, in Bantia's heights,
   Or on the rich plains of Forentum,
      All of them marveling

How I slept on, safe from bears and vipers,
How I had been draped with the sacred laurel
   And tender myrtle, a fearless child
      Favored by the gods.

Yours, my Muses, I am yours whenever I climb
The lofty Sabine hills, or when cool Praeneste,
   Hillside Tibur, or glimmering Baiae
      Takes my fancy.

Devoted to your springs and choral dances,
I escaped unharmed in the rout at Philippi,
   Escaped that cursèd falling tree
      And the shipwreck off Sicily.

utcumque mecum vos eritis, libens
insanientem navita Bosphorum
  temptabo et urentes harenas
    litoris Assyrii viator;

visam Britannos hospitibus feros
et laetum equino sanguine Concanum,
  visam pharetratos Gelonos
    et Scythicum inviolatus amnem.

vos Caesarem altum, militia simul
fessas cohortes addidit oppidis,
  finire quaerentem labores,
    Pierio recreatis antro.

vos lene consilium et datis et dato
gaudetis, almae. scimus, ut impios
  Titanas immanemque turbam
    fulmine sustulerit caduco,

qui terram inertem, qui mare temperat
ventosum et urbes regnaque tristia,
  divosque mortalesque turmas
    imperio regit unus aequo.

magnum illa terrorem intulerat Iovi
fidens iuventus horrida bracchiis
  fratresque tendentes opaco
    Pelion imposuisse Olympo.

sed quid Typhoeus et validus Mimas,
aut quid minaci Porphyrion statu,
  quid Rhoetus evulsisque truncis
    Enceladus iaculator audax

contra sonantem Palladis aegida
possent ruentes? hinc avidus stetit
  Vulcanus, hinc matrona Iuno et
    numquam umeris positurus arcum,

With you beside me, I would gladly set sail
Across the raging Bosphorus, or set forth
  Across the burning desert sands
    Of the Syrian shore.

I would visit the Britons, so savage to strangers,
And the Concanians who drink the blood of horses,
  Visit unharmed the Gelonians with their quivers,
    Or the roaring Scythian river.

You it is who, amidst the Pierian grottos, refresh
Even great Augustus when he would soothe his cares,
  Having disbanded his battle-spent legions
    And safely quartered them.

You it is, gentle spirits, who give mild counsel
And delight in the gift. We know full well
  How the brutal mob of impious Titans
    Was struck by thunderbolts

Thrown by him who alone rules the lifeless earth,
The wind-swept seas, the cities above and realms
  Of the dead below, who governs gods and men
    Alike in his supremacy.

A frightening terror they inflicted on Jove, that mob,
That hundred-handed monster, and the brothers
  Who strove to pile Mount Pelion
    Onto misty Olympus.

But how could the mightiest of Titans prevail,
Their threatening kings and bristling champions,
  Brandishing uprooted trees,
    Hurling themselves

Against the ringing shield of the goddess Minerva?
On one side stood Vulcan, coarse and panting,
  And on the other, the lady Juno and he
    Who never lays his bow aside,

qui rore puro Castaliae lavit
crines solutos, qui Lyciae tenet
   dumeta natalemque silvam,
      Delius et Patareus Apollo.

vis consili expers mole ruit sua:
vim temperatam di quoque provehunt
   in maius; idem odere vires
      omne nefas animo moventes.

testis mearum centimanus Gyas
sententiarum, notus et integrae
   temptator Orion Dianae,
      virginea domitus sagitta.

iniecta monstris Terra dolet suis
maeretque partus fulmine luridum
   missos ad Orcum; nec peredit
      impositam celer ignis Aetnen,

incontinentis nec Tityi iecur
reliquit ales, nequitiae additus
   custos; amatorem trecentae
      Pirithoum cohibent catenae.

Who bathes his unbound hair in the waters of Castalia,
Who haunts the thickets of Lycia and rules
   His native woodland, of Delos and Patara
      Lord, Apollo himself.

Force without wisdom falls by its own weight.
Power tempered with judgment the gods exalt.
   But they likewise abhor the violence
      That turns a heart to crime.

Let grasping Gyges be proof now of my verdict,
And Orion, notorious as chaste Diana's assailant,
   But struck down by her virginal arrow.
      The earth, slumped over

Her monstrous offspring, moans and mourns for
Her sons hurled by lightning down, down
   To the ashen underworld. The swift flames
      Have not yet eaten through Etna,

Nor has the vulture, once set on the criminal,
Done yet with the liver of lustful Tityos,
   And three hundred chains still hold
      Pirithous the adulterer.

J. D. McClatchy

III.5

Caelo tonantem credidimus Iovem
regnare; praesens divus habebitur
    Augustus adiectis Britannis
        imperio gravibusque Persis.

milesne Crassi coniuge barbara
turpis maritus vixit et hostium
    (pro curia inversique mores!)
        consenuit socerorum in armis

sub rege Medo, Marsus et Apulus
anciliorum et nominis et togae
    oblitus aeternaeque Vestae,
        incolumi Iove et urbe Roma?

hoc caverat mens provida Reguli
dissentientis condicionibus
    foedis et exemplo trahentis
        perniciem veniens in aevum,

si non periret immiserabilis
captiva pubes. "signa ego Punicis
    adfixa delubris et arma
        militibus sine caede" dixit

"derepta vidi, vidi ego civium
retorta tergo bracchia libero
    portasque non clausas et arva
        Marte coli populata nostro.

auro repensus scilicet acrior
miles redibit. flagitio additis
    damnum: neque amissos colores
        lana refert medicata fuco,

III.5

The heavens that echo with his thundering
Convince us: indeed Jupiter is king.
Conqueror of Britons and of Persians too,
Augustus now is godlike here below.
But customs, politics—all heels over head
Turn, topsy-turvy. Crassus' soldiers wed
Enemy girls, wear out their fighting lives
Siding with the fathers of their wives,
Serving as subjects of the Persian king,
Forgetting their own names, and everything
Else that confers Roman identity—
Vesta, the sacred shields, and Jove triumphant in the sky.

Regulus feared just this would come to pass
When he refused a peace that spelled disgrace,
Forseeing ruin on the road ahead
Unless young prisoners, unpitied, died.
"Our troops surrendering with no blood shed;
Our eagles punctured by the Punic sword,
All this," said Regulus, "my eyes have seen.
The gates of Carthage open once again;
Romans taken prisoner; fields we'd sown
With salt grown once more fertile, lush, and green—
These I have witnessed. Do you think a man
Ransomed with gold will risk his neck again
In battle? Onto shame you pile defeat.
Wool once dyed purple won't return to white.

nec vera virtus, cum semel excidit,
curat reponi deterioribus.
    si pugnat extricata densis
       cerva plagis, erit ille fortis

qui perfidis se credidit hostibus,
et Marte Poenos proteret altero,
    qui lora restrictis lacertis
       sensit iners timuitque mortem.

hic, unde vitam sumeret inscius,
pacem duello miscuit. o pudor!
    o magna Carthago, probrosis
       altior Italiae ruinis!"

fertur pudicae coniugis osculum
parvosque natos ut capitis minor
    ab se removisse et virilem
       torvus humi posuisse voltum,

donec labantis consilio patres
firmaret auctor numquam alias dato,
    interque maerentes amicos
       egregius properaret exsul.

atqui sciebat quae sibi barbarus
tortor pararet. non aliter tamen
    dimovit obstantes propinquos
       et populum reditus morantem,

quam si clientum longa negotia
diiudicata lite relinqueret,
    tendens Venafranos in agros
       aut Lacedaemonium Tarentum.

When manhood, courage, virtue once depart,
They don't return; things start to fall apart.
I'd just as soon expect a doe to fight—
One that has managed to escape a net—
As hope a Roman soldier, once he has
Trusted his skin to treacherous enemies,
Will burst with valor, strive for victory
In one more war. When once the enemy
Prevails, this paragon of virtue stands
Terrified, trembling, helpless, with bound hands.
Hoping to survive a few years more,
He's ignorantly confounded peace with war."

As if deprived of citizenship, it's said,
Regulus stepped aside and turned his head
Away from wife and children, their embrace,
And stared down at the ground, till his advice
(Unheard-of plan) should finally put strength
Into the weak-kneed Senate. But at length
He pushed his way through crowds who stood between
Him and the noblest exile ever seen.
What tortures were awaiting him he knew
Perfectly well; but hurried out as though,
Finally free of tedious hours in court,
Demanding clients, he were heading out
To some secluded valley, cool and green,
Some innocent and peaceful little town.

Rachel Hadas

III.6

Delicta maiorum immeritus lues,
Romane, donec templa refeceris
   aedesque labentes deorum et
      foeda nigro simulacra fumo.

dis te minorem quod geris, imperas:
hinc omne principium; huc refer exitum.
   di multa neglecti dederunt
      Hesperiae mala luctuosae.

iam bis Monaeses et Pacori manus
non auspicatos contudit impetus
   nostros et adiecisse praedam
      torquibus exiguis renidet.

paene occupatam seditionibus
delevit urbem Dacus et Aethiops,
   hic classe formidatus, ille
      missilibus melior sagittis.

fecunda culpae saecula nuptias
primum inquinavere et genus et domos:
   hoc fonte derivata clades
      in patriam populumque fluxit.

motus doceri gaudet Ionicos
matura virgo et fingitur artibus
   iam nunc et incestos amores
      de tenero meditatur ungui

mox iuniores quaerit adulteros
inter mariti vina, neque eligit
   cui donet impermissa raptim
      gaudia luminibus remotis,

III.6

Whatever *you* did or did not do, Romans,
    you shall atone for your fathers' sins.
Crumbling temples must be rebuilt, altars
made worthy of the sacrifice restored.

Once you ruled by religion; honor your gods—
    they were the beginning, they will be
the end. Neglected, they will perpetrate
horror after horror on Hesperia.

Twice already the armies of Monaeses
    and Pacorus have defeated ours,
and brag of adding to their paltry loot
the eagles of Roman legions! Rome

herself, weakened by sedition, was almost
    overrun by Ethiopians—
helpless against their fleet and their allies,
Dacian archers with invincible shafts.

Ours is a lineage that knows not the law:
    marriages, children, hearths defiled,
and from this source come all catastrophes,
vanquishing our people and our very earth.

Young women clamor to learn the bad Greek ways,
    lascivious dances are the rage,
each "virgin," to her painted fingernails,
is overcome by profligate desire.

At parties, a wife works the room for partners
    younger than her complicit husband:
a sailor, a salesman—any lust will do,
all new lovers being equal in the dark.

sed iussa coram non sine conscio
surgit marito, seu vocat institor
    seu navis Hispanae magister,
        dedecorum pretiosus emptor.

non his iuventus orta parentibus
infecit aequor sanguine Punico
    Pyrrhumque et ingentem cecidit
        Antiochum Hannibalemque dirum;

sed rusticorum mascula militum
proles, Sabellis docta ligonibus
    versare glaebas et severae
        matris ad arbitrium recisos

portare fustes, Sol ubi montium
mutaret umbras et iuga demeret
    bobus fatigatis, amicum
        tempus agens abeunte curru.

damnosa quid non imminuit dies?
aetas parentum, peior avis, tulit
    nos nequiores, mox daturos
        progeniem vitiosiorem.

Not so the sires of youth that rouged . . . the *sea*
    with Punic blood, left Pyrrhus for dead,
destroyed great Herod and dread Hannibal,
and yet were taught to wield the Sabine hoe,

to plough a father's fields and carry logs
    to a waiting mother at sunset
while shadows spread across the hills: an hour
of welcome rest for oxen as for men.

What has Time left intact? Lesser than their own,
    our parents bore children lesser still,
and ours are lesser still than we, and theirs
than they. And theirs again than they . . .

                    Richard Howard

III.7

Quid fles, Asterie, quem tibi candidi
primo restituent vere Favonii
    Thyna merce beatum,
        constantis iuvenem fide,

Gygen? ille Notis actus ad Oricum
post insana Caprae sidera frigidas
    noctes non sine multis
        insomnis lacrimis agit.

atqui sollicitae nuntius hospitae,
suspirare Chloen et miseram tuis
    dicens ignibus uri,
        temptat mille vafer modis.

ut Proetum mulier perfida credulum
falsis impulerit criminibus nimis
    casto Bellerophontae
        maturare necem refert;

narrat paene datum Pelea Tartaro,
Magnessam Hippolyten dum fugit abstinens;
    et peccare docentes
        fallax historias movet.

frustra: nam scopulis surdior Icari
voces audit adhuc integer. at tibi
    ne vicinus Enipeus
        plus iusto placeat cave;

quamvis non alius flectere equum sciens
aeque conspicitur gramine Martio,
    ne quisquam citus aeque
        Tusco denatat alveo.

prima nocte domum claude neque in vias
sub cantu querulae despice tibiae,
    et te saepe vocanti
        duram difficilis mane.

III.7

Why are you crying, Asteria, for Gyges
when the bright west winds will bring him home in spring
    flush from deals in Bithynia
        and always faithful to you?

Under the crazed Goat Star, the south wind drove him
to Oricum, where he shivers through the nights,
    insomniac, cold, dampening
        his pillow with tears.

But that sly servant girl sidles up and murmurs
how Chloë, his love-dazed hostess, pines for him,
    and burns with your very fires—
        in a thousand ways, the girl tempts him.

She tells how his treacherous wife pushed Proetus,
who fell for her lying stories and accusations,
    to plot revenge upon
        too-chaste Bellerophon;

she tells how Peleus almost plunged to the Underworld
for keeping his hands off Magnessian Hippolyte;
    and with every breath, the vixen
        instructs him how to sin.

Don't worry: your Gyges, deafer than the Icarian cliff,
hears all this and, so far, stands firm. But you,
    my dear, watch that your neighbor Enipeus
        doesn't charm you more than he should;

though he's the most dashing rider on the Field of Mars,
the most elegant horseman, and no one swims so well
    the Tiber's powerful current
        in the public view.

As soon as night falls, bolt your shutters and doors, and don't
peek out in the street at the tune of his pleading flute;
    hold firm, no matter how
        often he calls you cruel.

Rosanna Warren

III.8

Martiis caelebs quid agam Kalendis,
quid velint flores et acerra turis
plena miraris positusque carbo in
    caespite vivo,

docte sermones utriusque linguae.
voveram dulces epulas et album
Libero caprum prope funeratus
    arboris ictu.

hic dies anno redeunte festus
corticem adstrictum pice demovebit
amphorae fumum bibere institutae
    consule Tullo.

sume, Maecenas, cyathos amici
sospitis centum et vigiles lucernas
perfer in lucem: procul omnis esto
    clamor et ira.

mitte civiles super urbe curas:
occidit Daci Cotisonis agmen,
Medus infestus sibi luctuosis
    dissidet armis,

servit Hispanae vetus hostis orae
Cantaber, sera domitus catena,
iam Scythae laxo meditantur arcu
    cedere campis.

neglegens, ne qua populus laboret,
parce privatus nimium cavere et
dona praesentis cape laetus horae ac
    linque severa.

III.8

What's up, the start of March, the Matronalia, unmarried man
That I am, flowers everywhere, little box of incense,
Fresh coals laid out on fresh-cut turf?
Well you might ask

Versed as you are in Greek and Latin rituals.
I vowed to Bacchus a white goat and a big feast
Each year after that tree fell and just about
Funeraled me.

This is the first anniversary of the vow,
The first feast, and I've got a wine jar
Smoke-sealed and aged from Tullus's time I'm set
To break the pitch on and uncork.

So, Maecenas, let's drink a hundred cups
To the safety of your friend, and keep the lamps lit
Till the dawn's light, and let there be
No rancor, no anger.

Let loose, for a while, of your worries about the state:
Cotiso and the Dacians are done for,
The Mede inflicts his own wounds on himself
In a civil war,

The Cantabriani along the Spanish coast
Now rattle their Roman chains at last,
And the Scythians, their bows unstrung, move north,
Leaving the plains.

So settle down, stop worrying whether or not
The public is satisfied, relax,
Take on the mantle of pleasure when it's offered,
Don't be so serious all the time.

Charles Wright

III.9

"Donec gratus eram tibi
  nec quisquam potior bracchia candidae
cervici iuvenis dabat,
  Persarum vigui rege beatior."

"donec non alia magis
  arsisti neque erat Lydia post Chloen,
multi Lydia nominis
  Romana vigui clarior Ilia."

"me nunc Thressa Chloe regit,
  dulces docta modos et citharae sciens,
pro qua non metuam mori,
  si parcent animae fata superstiti."

"me torret face mutua
  Thurini Calais filius Ornyti,
pro quo bis patiar mori,
  si parcent puero fata superstiti."

"quid si prisca redit Venus
  diductosque iugo cogit aëneo?
si flava excutitur Chloe
  reiectaeque patet ianua Lydiae?"

"quamquam sidere pulchrior
  ille est, tu levior cortice et improbo
iracundior Hadria,
  tecum vivere amem, tecum obeam libens!"

III.9

When I was wound round luminous
you more tightly than you'd let
anyone else dare dream of,
I was a pasha, I was in bliss.

Before your flame for your Lydia
leapt to some second-place person,
leaving me cold as yesterday's news,
I was in splendor, I was a star.

A fierce girl lords it over me now,
a musician; she plays me like her lyre:
I'd give my life gladly if she,
precious she, were permitted to live.

My fire's fused with a fine young
someone else; you'd know his name:
I'd die twice if he, dear,
dear boy, were allotted long life.

What if some god of love came along
to nail back what's fallen asunder?
If I showed today's darling the door,
would long-lost Lydia enter?

My sweetheart's as lovely as starlight,
while you, you seethe like the sea,
and you're fickle as foam, but yes,
enter Lydia: without you I die.

C. K. Williams

III. 10

Extremum Tanain si biberes, Lyce,
saevo nupta viro, me tamen asperas
porrectum ante fores obicere incolis
    plorares Aquilonibus.

audis, quo strepitu ianua, quo nemus
inter pulchra satum tecta remugiat
ventis, et positas ut glaciet nives
    puro numine Iuppiter?

ingratam Veneri pone superbiam,
ne currente retro funis eat rota:
non te Penelopen difficilem procis
    Tyrrhenus genuit parens.

o quamvis neque te munera nec preces
nec tinctus viola pallor amantium
nec vir Pieria paelice saucius
    curvat, supplicibus tuis

parcas, nec rigida mollior aesculo
nec Mauris animum mitior anguibus.
non hoc semper erit liminis aut aquae
    caelestis patiens latus.

If you lived as wild as a wolf by the river
that runs at the roaring end of the world
with a husband as savage as you, you'd still weep
to see me shiver like this on your step.

Can't you hear the hinges of the gate howl,
and the courtyard trees cry in the tempest?
The holy heavens are cruelly, bitterly clear,
and so cold they're crusting the new-sown snow.

Don't be so disdainful: take up your end
of the rope in love's sweet tug of war;
your parents were real, they weren't rearing
some fanatically faithful Penelope myth.

Please, if my presents don't persuade you,
nor my prayers, or pallor (nor, by the way,
that your husband is off somewhere with his whore),
at least have pity on your pathetic admirers.

You might be as tough as a tree and about
as amiable as an asp; don't think, though,
that frail flesh can withstand such showers
of abuse: I won't be your doormat forever.

C. K. Williams

III.11

Mercuri (nam te docilis magistro
movit Amphion lapides canendo),
tuque testudo resonare septem
    callida nervis,

nec loquax olim neque grata, nunc et
divitum mensis et amica templis,
dic modos, Lyde quibus obstinatas
    applicet aures,

quae velut latis equa trima campis
ludit exsultim metuitque tangi,
nuptiarum expers et adhuc protervo
    cruda marito.

tu potes tigres comitesque silvas
ducere et rivos celeres morari;
cessit immanis tibi blandienti
    ianitor aulae,

Cerberus, quamvis furiale centum
muniant angues caput eius atque
spiritus taeter saniesque manet
    ore trilingui.

quin et Ixion Tityosque voltu
risit invito, stetit urna paulum
sicca, dum grato Danai puellas
    carmine mulces.

audiat Lyde scelus atque notas
virginum poenas et inane lymphae
dolium fundo pereuntis imo
    seraque fata,

quae manent culpas etiam sub Orco.
impiae (nam quid potuere maius?)
impiae sponsos potuere duro
    perdere ferro.

III.11

Mercury, old teacher, you who taught
Amphion to move stones with his music,
and you, my lyre, made of tortoise shell,
whose seven strings a short time ago

were neither in tune nor worth a listen,
but now are all the rage
in the temples of the gods
and where the rich dine in style:

Play something to make young Lyde
lend an ear as she skips about
in her short skirt, whinnying
still to be mounted by some eager boy.

You have the power to charm tigers and trees
to walk in your footsteps and to halt
a rushing brook. Even Cerberus,
who guards the manhole to hell,

lay down with a sigh, a tangle of snakes
crowning his hideous head,
foul breath and gore oozing
down his three lolling tongues.

Even Ixion and Tityos grinned
through their torment, the urn stayed dry
briefly as your dreamy tune
enthralled the daughters of Danaus.

Let Lyde hear the story of the crimes
these bitches committed and of their punishment,
how their urn never fills up with water
but leaks its contents out of the bottom,

and of the fate that awaits their kind
where death runs the show. These wicked brides
put knives to their husbands' throats
as they closed their eyes in bliss.

una de multis face nuptiali
digna periurum fuit in parentem
splendide mendax et in omne virgo
    nobilis aevum,

"surge" quae dixit iuveni marito,
"surge, ne longus tibi somnus, unde
non times, detur; socerum et scelestas
    falle sorores,

quae, velut nanctae vitulos leaenae,
singulos eheu lacerant: ego illis
mollior nec te feriam neque intra
    claustra tenebo.

me pater saevis oneret catenis,
quod viro clemens misero peperci;
me vel extremos Numidarum in agros
    classe releget.

i, pedes quo te rapiunt et aurae,
dum favet Nox et Venus; i secundo
omine, et nostri memorem sepulcro
    scalpe querellam."

One alone among them was worthy
of the marriage vows. Deftly
she tricked her crazed father.
May her memory live forever.

"Arise before you give up the ghost,"
she said to her bridegroom. "Flee my sisters.
They are like lionesses now, tearing
The flesh of a young steer they've seized.

I'm of a gentle heart. I'll neither cut you
nor keep you under lock and key.
Let my father bind me with heavy chains
for the pity I've shown to you.

Let me sail into banishment,
end up in some African desert.
Go wherever your feet
and the night breezes take you

while Venus and darkness consent.
Go with my blessing
and in my memory carve
some sad verses upon my empty sepulcher."

Charles Simic

III.12

Miserarum est neque amori dare ludum neque dulci
mala vino lavere aut exanimari metuentes
    patruae verbera linguae.

tibi qualum Cythereae puer ales, tibi telas
operosaeque Minervae studium aufert, Neobule,
    Liparaei nitor Hebri

simul unctos Tiberinis umeros lavit in undis,
eques ipso melior Bellerophonte, neque pugno
    neque segni pede victus,

catus idem per apertum fugientes agitato
grege cervos iaculari et celer arto latitantem
    fruticeto excipere aprum.

III.12

Poor girls! indoors, never outdoors,
with no love-games and no wine-cup
and old daddy's brother Sharp-Tongue keeping watch.

Neobule, you're in danger.
Cupid's flown off with your work-stuff.
Good Minerva will abhor you,
now you've seen him: gorgeous Hebrus,

just his shoulder, oiled and thrusting
wet and streaming from the river—
he's a runner and a boxer unbeaten
and on horseback he's just brilliant.

When he's hunting he can spear deer
though they scatter every which way;
he can winkle out the wild boar
hidden safe in thickest thickets, when he wants.

Marie Ponsot

III.13

O fons Bandusiae, splendidior vitro,
dulci digne mero non sine floribus,
   cras donaberis haedo,
      cui frons turgida cornibus

primis et venerem et proelia destinat.
frustra: nam gelidos inficiet tibi
   rubro sanguine rivos
      lascivi suboles gregis.

te flagrantis atrox hora Caniculae
nescit tangere, tu frigus amabile
   fessis vomere tauris
      praebes et pecori vago.

fies nobilium tu quoque fontium,
me dicente cavis impositam ilicem
   saxis, unde loquaces
      lymphae desiliunt tuae.

Bold as crystal, bright as glass
Your waters leap while we appear
Carrying to your woodland shrine
Gifts below your worthiness,
Grape and flower, Bandusia,
yellow hawksbeard, ready wine.

And tomorrow we will bring
A struggling kid, its temples sore
With early horns, as sacrifice.
Tomorrow its new trumpeting
Will come to nothing when its gore
Stains and thaws your bright ice.

Canicula, the lamp of drought,
The summer's fire, leaves your grace
Inviolate in the woods where
Every day you spring to comfort
The broad bull in his trace,
The herd out of the shepherd's care.

With every fountain, every spring
Of legend I will set you down
In praise and immortal spate.
These waters which drop gossiping
To ground, this wet surrounding stone
And this green oak I celebrate.

Eavan Boland

III.14

Herculis ritu modo dictus, o plebs,
morte venalem petiisse laurum
Caesar Hispana repetit penates
    victor ab ora.

unico gaudens mulier marito
prodeat iustis operata divis
et soror clari ducis et decorae
    supplice vitta

virginum matres iuvenumque nuper
sospitum. vos, o pueri et puellae
non virum expertae, maleominatis
    parcite verbis.

hic dies vere mihi festus atras
eximet curas; ego nec tumultum
nec mori per vim metuam tenente
    Caesare terras.

i, pete unguentum, puer, et coronas
et cadum Marsi memorem duelli,
Spartacum siqua potuit vagantem
    fallere testa.

dic et argutae properet Neaerae
murreum nodo cohibere crinem;
si per invisum mora ianitorem
    fiet, abito.

lenit albescens animos capillus
litium et rixae cupidos protervae;
non ego hoc ferrem calidus iuventa
    consule Planco.

III.14

Our Caesar, our Hercules, they said
he'd die earning this laurel, but he returns
from the shores of Spain, to us, to his hearth,
　　his own household

—joyful welcome! After the glad offerings
his wife and sister lead the procession,
wearing the crowns of prayer, their children
　　saved from war:

the returning heroes, the new brides.
You, you young boys and girls, don't say
a word to mar the formal moment,
　　keep quiet now.

For me this festive day ends
my cares; I won't be afraid of civil war
or a violent death, not while Caesar's
　　here on earth.

Go, boy, bring perfume, and wreaths,
and a jar of old wine from the years
of the Marsian wars, if any's survived
　　the rebellions.

And tell Neara, with her fine, clear voice,
to put up her chestnut hair, and hurry here!
Though if that cranky doorkeeper causes trouble,
　　let her be.

Back when Planco was consul, I'd never
have taken an insult like that—but as my hair's
gone white my spirit's calmed, and I've lost
　　my will for brawling.

Mark Doty

III.15

Uxor pauperis Ibyci,
    tandem nequitiae fige modum tuae
famosisque laboribus;
    maturo propior desine funeri

inter ludere virgines
    et stellis nebulam spargere candidis.
non, si quid Pholoen, satis
    et te, Chlori, decet: filia rectius

expugnat iuvenum domos,
    pulso Thyias uti concita tympano.
illam cogit amor Nothi
    lascivae similem ludere capreae;

te lanae prope nobilem
    tonsae Luceriam, non citharae decent
nec flos purpureus rosae
    nec poti vetulam faece tenus cadi.

III.15

Wife of Ibycus, man of small fortune,
stop your little games. At your age,
   Chloris, it's time to give up
sporting around. You're about ready

   for the grave, so don't behave
as if you were one of the randy girls,
   and darken their sky
with your sluttishness. Your daughter Pholoë

   chases handsome boys
as well she might, pursuing them into their villas.
   Roused by drums like a Bacchante,
she's a nanny goat in her lust for Nothus.

   But for you, at your age, it's time
to spin Luceria's wool. Forget love songs,
   Chloris. Stop dreaming of roses
—and stop drinking great jars of wine all day.

Donald Hall

III.16

Inclusam Danaën turris aënea
robustaeque fores et vigilum canum
tristes excubiae munierant satis
    nocturnis ab adulteris,

si non Acrisium virginis abditae
custodem pavidum Iuppiter et Venus
risissent: fore enim tutum iter et patens
    converso in pretium deo.

aurum per medios ire satellites
et perrumpere amat saxa, potentius
ictu fulmineo: concidit auguris
    Argivi domus, ob lucrum

demersa exitio; diffidit urbium
portas vir Macedo et subruit aemulos
reges muneribus; munera navium
    saevos inlaqueant duces.

crescentem sequitur cura pecuniam
maiorumque fames. iure perhorrui
late conspicuum tollere verticem,
    Maecenas, equitum decus.

quanto quisque sibi plura negaverit,
ab dis plura feret: nil cupientium
nudus castra peto et transfuga divitum
    partes linquere gestio,

contemptae dominus splendidior rei,
quam si, quidquid arat impiger Apulus,
occultare meis dicerer horreis,
    magnas inter opes inops.

III.16

Acrisius, Danaë's fearful father—
Whose banal tower of bronze and oaken portal
And trained attack dogs had been meant to keep
His virgin from a midnight lover—

Made Jupiter and Venus jeer and scoff.
They realized that once the god had changed
Himself to gold dust, infiltration
Would simply be unstoppable.

Gold loves to work its way through famous safeguards—
Or, as lightning, to fracture mortised stones.
The Argive's house itself was struck by lucre,
Then rapidly dilapidated.

Likewise Philip's great bribes pried the gates
Of cities open and blew to shards and flinders
Opponents' claims, while money roiled the seas
And snared fierce admirals as well.

As wealth accumulates, anxiety
Mounts too. And greed. I knew what I was doing,
Maecenas, who styled yourself a horseman merely,
When I maintained my own low profile.

In just the measure one abstains, the gods
Bestow their gifts. Unarmed myself, I must
Desert the moneyed ranks to join the poor
Camp of the richly satisfied,

To be a lord of *more* than one who buys
And hoards the grain—the grain the peasant worked
So hard to cultivate—then stands alone,
A scarecrow, amid fertility.

purae rivus aquae silvaque iugerum
paucorum et segetis certa fides meae
fulgentem imperio fertilis Africae
    fallit sorte beatior.

quamquam nec Calabrae mella ferunt apes,
nec Laestrygonia Bacchus in amphora
languescit mihi, nec pinguia Gallicis
    crescunt vellera pascuis:

importuna tamen pauperies abest,
nec si plura velim tu dare deneges.
contracto melius parva cupidine
    vectigalia porrigam,

quam si Mygdoniis regnum Alyattei
campis continuem. multa petentibus
desunt multa; bene est, cui deus obtulit
    parca quod satis est manu.

Pure water from my simple woodland's stream
And crops I can rely on make me more
Comfortable than any potentate
In fecund Africa can be.

Bees from Calabria do not make honey
For me, nor does Bacchus lay away
For me his vintage wines, nor do the Gauls
Card and spin fine wool for me.

Still, I'm far from destitute. And if
I needed more, I'm sure you would comply.
In any case, I think I can increase
By husbandry my modest profits

Beyond the profits of the covetous
Provincial princes. And it's the greediest
Who gleans at last the least. Who asks at first
The minimum is blest the most.

Stephen Yenser

Aeli vetusto nobilis ab Lamo,
quando et priores hinc Lamias ferunt
   denominatos et nepotum
      per memores genus omne fastos;

auctore ab illo ducis originem,
qui Formiarum moenia dicitur
   princeps et innantem Maricae
      litoribus tenuisse Lirim,

late tyrannus. cras foliis nemus
multis et alga litus inutili
   demissa tempestas ab Euro
      sternet, aquae nisi fallit augur

annosa cornix. dum potes, aridum
compone lignum; cras Genium mero
   curabis et porco bimenstri
      cum famulis operum solutis.

III. 17

Aelius Lamia, son of a legend—
That legendary Lamus from whom came
The ancient Lamiae and all the others who
    Followed on later and took their name

From him for all time—your ancestor
Was a brute-king who ruled over the walls
Of the city of Formia and the river Liris where
    It rises up and floods Marica's shore.

Unless our old prophet of rain is wrong—
Our old raven—tomorrow will surely bring
A tempest from the east, a wild storm.
    The woods will be knee-deep in leaves.

The shore will be strewn with useless seaweed.
So gather your kindling while you can! Tomorrow, pray
Have a suckling pig and soothe your good soul
    With unwatered wine and take your ease—

With even your slaves off for the day.

Eavan Boland

III.18

Faune, Nympharum fugientum amator,
per meos fines et aprica rura
lenis incedas abeasque parvis
    aequus alumnis,

si tener pleno cadit haedus anno,
larga nec desunt Veneris sodali
vina craterae, vetus ara multo
    fumat odore.

ludit herboso pecus omne campo,
cum tibi nonae redeunt Decembres;
festus in pratis vacat otioso
    cum bove pagus;

inter audaces lupus errat agnos;
spargit agrestis tibi silva frondes;
gaudet invisam pepulisse fossor
    ter pede terram.

III.18

Faunus, you who love the nymphs, from whom the nymphs love to run,
may you look kindly, as you cross in and out of my farm,
on its boundary-posts and pastures already blessed by the sun,
and deliver the littlest of my flock from harm

if it please you that, at the high point of the year,
a little kid might indeed be offered to you, the wine
which Venus holds so dear
indeed fill the mixing-bowl, smoke rise from the ancient shrine,

one and all besporting themselves on the still-green grazing
as early December rolls round, be it the flocks
of sheep or the country folk lazing
with the lazing ox,

the wolf moving among lambs remarkable for their nonchalance,
the trees putting out their red
carpet for you, or the ditchdigger dancing a three-step victory dance
on the earth with which he's gone head-to-head.

Paul Muldoon

III.19

Quantum distet ab Inacho
    Codrus pro patria non timidus mori
narras et genus Aeaci
    et pugnata sacro bella sub Ilio;

quo Chium pretio cadum
    mercemur, quis aquam temperet ignibus,
quo praebente domum et quota
    Paelignis caream frigoribus, taces.

da lunae propere novae,
    da noctis mediae, da, puer, auguris
Murenae: tribus aut novem
    miscentur cyathis pocula commodis.

qui Musas amat impares,
    ternos ter cyathos attonitus petet
vates; tres prohibet supra
    rixarum metuens tangere Gratia

nudis iuncta sororibus.
    insanire iuvat: cur Berecyntiae
cessant flamina tibiae?
    cur pendet tacita fistula cum lyra?

parcentes ego dexteras
    odi: sparge rosas; audiat invidus
dementem strepitum Lycus
    et vicina seni non habilis Lyco.

spissa te nitidum coma,
    puro te similem, Telephe, vespero
tempestiva petit Rhode;
    me lentus Glycerae torret amor meae.

III.19

You talk very well about Inachus,
    And Codrus, unafraid to die for his city,
And the offspring of old Aeacus
    And the fighting at sacred Ilium under the walls,

But on the price of Chian wine,
    And the question of who's going to warm it,
Under whose roof it will be drunk,
    And when my bones will come unfrozen, you are mute.

Boy, let's drink to the new moon's sliver,
    And drink to the middle of the night, and drink
To good Murena, with three glasses
    Or with nine. Nine, says the madman poet

Whom the uneven-numbered Muses love.
    Three, says the even-tempered Grace who holds
Her naked sisters by the hands
    And disapproves altogether of brawling,

Should do a party handsomely.
    But what I want's to rave. Why is the flute
From Phrygia silent? Why are the lyre
    And the reed pipe hanging on the wall?

Oh, how I hate a pinching hand.
    Scatter the roses! Let jealous old Lycus
Listen to our pandemonium,
    And also that pretty neighbor he's not up to.

Rhoda loves your locks, Telephus.
    She thinks they glisten like the evening star.
As for me, I'm still stuck on Glycera:
    with a love that smoulders in me like slow fire.

Robert Hass

III.20

Non vides, quanto moveas periclo,
Pyrrhe, Gaetulae catulos leaenae?
dura post paulo fugies inaudax
    proelia raptor,

cum per obstantes iuvenum catervas
ibit insignem repetens Nearchum:
grande certamen, tibi praeda cedat,
    maior an illi.

interim, dum tu celeres sagittas
promis, haec dentes acuit timendos,
arbiter pugnae posuisse nudo
    sub pede palmam

fertur et leni recreare vento
sparsum odoratis umerum capillis,
qualis aut Nireus fuit aut aquosa
    raptus ab Ida.

III.20

Don't you see, Pyrrhus, how risky it is
to disturb an African lionness's cubs?
Soon enough, you trembling plunderer, you'll run
    from harsh battles

when she breaks through the protective ranks of boys
looking for Nearchus, stark in his nimbus of beauty:
a great contest, to see where the reward falls,
    to you or to her.

Meanwhile, as you draw your swift arrows out
of the quiver, and she sharpens her fearful teeth,
the judge, and prize, of the fight stands casually
    with his bare foot

on the victory palm, letting the sweet breeze
play round his shoulders in a tumble of perfumed hair,
like Nireus, or like lovely Ganymede stolen
    from Ida's streams.

                  Rosanna Warren

III.21

O nata mecum consule Manlio,
seu tu querellas sive geris iocos
    seu rixam et insanos amores
        seu facilem, pia testa, somnum,

quocumque lectum nomine Massicum
servas, moveri digna bono die,
    descende Corvino iubente
        promere languidiora vina.

non ille, quamquam Socraticis madet
sermonibus, te negleget horridus:
    narratur et prisci Catonis
        saepe mero caluisse virtus.

tu lene tormentum ingenio admoves
plerumque duro; tu sapientium
    curas et arcanum iocoso
        consilium retegis Lyaeo;

tu spem reducis mentibus anxiis
viresque et addis cornua pauperi,
    post te neque iratos trementi
        regum apices neque militum arma.

te Liber et si laeta aderit Venus
segnesque nodum solvere Gratiae
    vivaeque producent lucernae,
        dum rediens fugat astra Phoebus.

III.21

O *mise-en-bouteille* in the very year of my birth
And Manlius' consulship, celestial spirits,
Instinct with ardors, slugfests, the sighs of lovers,
Hilarity and effortless sleep, whatever,
Campanian harvest, well-sealed special reserve
For some fine and festive holiday, descend
From your high cellarage, since my friend, Corvinus,
A connoisseur, has called for a more mature wine.
Soaked though he be in vintage Socratic wisdom,
He's not going to snub you. For even Cato the Elder,
All Roman rectitude, would warm to a drink.

You limber the dullard's faculties with your proddings;
With Bacchus the Trickster you break through careful discretion,
Making even the politic say what they mean.
You resurrect hope in the most dejected of minds;
To the poor and weak you lend such measure of courage
As after a single gulp allays their palsy
When faced with the wrath of monarchs, or unsheathed weapons.
Bacchus and Venus (if she will condescend),
The arm-linked Graces in unclad sorority,
And vigil lamps will honor you all night long
Till Phoebus, with punctual bustle, banishes starlight.

Anthony Hecht

III.22

Montium custos nemorumque, Virgo,
quae laborantes utero puellas
ter vocata audis adimisque leto,
    diva triformis,

imminens villae tua pinus esto,
quam per exactos ego laetus annos
verris obliquum meditantis ictum
    sanguine donem.

Maiden-goddess
    guardian of these
      hills and groves,
when the cries—
    repeated thrice—
      of girl-mothers,
in the throes
    of birth and labor,
      reach your ears,
you hear their prayers,
you save their lives.
Three-sided goddess
    I offer this
    pine which overhangs
      my house.
    With a glad heart
through the years
    I will bring to it
      the wild, first
blood of a boar
      just beginning
to swerve and thrust.

Eavan Boland

III.23

Caelo supinas si tuleris manus
nascente luna, rustica Phidyle,
   si ture placaris et horna
      fruge Lares avidaque porca:

nec pestilentem sentiet Africum
fecunda vitis nec sterilem seges
   robiginem aut dulces alumni
      pomifero grave tempus anno.

nam quae nivali pascitur Algido
devota quercus inter et ilices
   aut crescit Albanis in herbis
      victima, pontificum securis

cervice tinguet: te nihil attinet
temptare multa caede bidentium
   parvos coronantem marino
      rore deos fragilique myrto.

immunis aram si tetigit manus,
non sumptuosa blandior hostia,
   mollivit aversos Penates
      farre pio et saliente mica.

Hold out your hands, girl, open
your palms to the moon, it's new,
   and new the grain and suckling
     pig you'll offer up with incense to

the gods. Do this with an open heart,
your vines will thrive, the pestilent
   scirocco will not wither them nor
     blight beset your corn, your lambs

will leap among the apple-burdened trees.
That creature grazing in the Alban
   Hills among the oak and ilex, he's
     already doomed, the neck

he bends to crop the grass is
destined for the ax. Leave axes
   to the priests, girl, and the lavish
     blood of full-grown sheep.

Crown your little deities with rosemary
and myrtle. A clean hand on the altar and
   a scattering of meal and salt
     are sweeter to the gods than gore.

Linda Gregerson

III.24

Intactis opulentior
    thesauris Arabum et divitis Indiae
caementis licet occupes
    terrenum omne tuis et mare publicum;

si figit adamantinos
    summis verticibus dira Necessitas
clavos, non animum metu,
    non mortis laqueis expedies caput.

campestres melius Scythae,
    quorum plaustra vagas rite trahunt domos,
vivunt et rigidi Getae,
    immetata quibus iugera liberas

fruges et Cererem ferunt,
    nec cultura placet longior annua,
defunctumque laboribus
    aequali recreat sorte vicarius.

illie matre carentibus
    privignis mulier temperat innocens,
nec dotata regit virum
    coniunx nec nitido fidit adultero.

dos est magna parentium
    virtus et metuens alterius viri
certo foedere castitas,
    et peccare nefas aut pretium est mori.

o quisquis volet impias
    caedes et rabiem tollere civicam,
si quaeret "Pater urbium"
    subscribi statuis, indomitam audeat

refrenare licentiam,
    clarus postgenitis: quatenus, heu nefas,
virtutem incolumem odimus,
    sublatam ex oculis quaerimus, invidi.

III.24

It simply makes no difference, Friend,
   Once Destiny has nailed your flesh and soul
Like common rafters to a king post,
   How opulent the mansion you yourself

Have built on jetties on the landfill
   Shoveled from ruins of some nearby villas,
How grand the view you have secured
   With right of way to public property.

It's better to have been a nomad,
   Or gypsy vendor always on the move,
Or freedman living in the outskirts,
   Or migrant laborer attendant on

The season only, still unmortgaged,
   Content to leave the well-worked premises
To others who will execute
   Faithfully the contracts that were signed.

Such workers take care of their orphans.
   They don't abuse them—nor do their luckier
Or blonder brides emasculate
   Their men or take up unctuous young lovers.

They hand down what their dauntless parents
   Husbanded, with fidelity,
To spouses and to steady friends.
   They know that perfidy amounts to death.

We need someone like one of them
   To end our civic riots, debauchery,
And prejudice, to curb at last
   This idiocy of license upon license.

Someone the future could call justly
   "Father of Cities" on commissioned statues
Might show the rest of us the way,
   The sycophants who otherwise worship

quid tristes querimoniae,
   si non supplicio culpa reciditur?
quid leges sine moribus
   vanae proficiunt? si neque fervidis

pars inclusa caloribus
   mundi nec Boreae finitimum latus
durataeque solo nives
   mercatorem abigunt, horrida callidi

vincunt aequora navitae,
   magnum pauperies opprobrium iubet
quidvis et facere et pati,
   virtutisque viam deserit arduae.

vel nos in Capitolium,
   quo clamor vocat et turba faventium,
vel nos in mare proximum
   gemmas et lapides aurum et inutile,

summi materiem mali,
   mittamus, scelerum si bene paenitet.
eradenda cupidinis
   pravi sunt elementa et tenerae nimis

mentes asperioribus
   formandae studiis. nescit equo rudis
haerere ingenuus puer
venarique timet, ludere doctior,

seu Graeco iubeas trocho,
   seu malis vetita legibus alea,
cum periura patris fides
   consortem socium fallat et hospites

indignoque pecuniam
   heredi properet. scilicet improbae
crescunt divitiae; tamen
   curtae nescio quid semper abest rei.

Morals only when they've died.
  What do recriminations matter if
Sanctions are not enforced? Or laws
  Themselves, absent simple integrity?

My friend, it simply makes no difference
  Whether we exploit the burning tropics,
Or colonize the freezing Arctic,
  Or sail out to the very ends of earth,

If fear of poverty itself
  Impoverish all of us by driving us,
From excess to excess, to shun
  Heartier climes of prudence and of justice.

We must redress our wrongs and prove
  Ourselves to an exultant multitude
By giving up our gold and jewels
  To charity—or dumping them at sea.

We must uproot materialism
  And avarice, which make us do our worst,
If we expect to scourge ourselves
  And discipline our deliquescent spirit.

No privileged child these days can ride
  A horse, he's so afraid of falling off,
Let alone spear a deer or boar.
  Instead he learns at home illicit games

Of chance or plays with balls or hoops,
  Those vestiges of precious Greek amusements.
Meanwhile his father lies, defrauds
  His friends, and piles up in his treasury

Illegal riches for his heir.
  The profits swell up like a pregnancy—
No, a tumor. They grow and grow—
  And must be terminated for our good.

Stephen Yenser

III.25

Quo me, Bacche, rapis tui
   plenum? quae nemora aut quos agor in specus,
velox mente nova? quibus
   antris egregii Caesaris audiar

aeternum meditans decus
   stellis inserere et consilio Iovis?
dicam insigne, recens, adhuc
   indictum ore alio. non secus in iugis

exsomnis stupet Euhias,
   Hebrum prospiciens et nive candidam
Thracen ac pede barbaro
   lustratam Rhodopen, ut mihi devio

ripas et vacuum nemus
   mirari libet. o Naiadum potens
Baccharumque valentium
   proceras manibus vertere fraxinos,

nil parvum aut humili modo,
   nil mortale loquar. dulce periculum est,
o Lenaee, sequi deum
   cingentem viridi tempora pampino.

Bacchus, where are you carrying me to
So spirited, so full of you?—
Driven to what woods, recesses,
My new-born vision scarcely guesses.
What echoing ravine will hear
My words enrolling star-god Caesar
In the heavenly senate? I shall sing
Some vigorous, unattempted thing,
Just like the Maenad who wakes up
Having blindly reached the mountain-top,
And wonders at the spread of space—
Dark River Hebrus, snow-clad Thrace,
The range that marks the Balkan frontier.
At rockscapes, woodland I, too, stare,
Grow dionysiac just like her.
Lord of the Naiads and Bacchantes
Who with bare hands uproot the trees,
Nothing little, low or mortal
Shall I sing now: I stand or fall,
Bacchus, beside the god who twines
His temples with the verdant vines.

Charles Tomlinson

Vixi Puellis nuper idoneus
et militavi non sine gloria;
　　nunc arma defunctumque bello
　　　barbiton hic paries habebit,

laevum marinae qui Veneris latus
custodit. hic, hic ponite lucida
　　funalia et vectes securesque
　　　oppositis foribus minaces.

o quae beatam diva tenes Cyprum et
Memphin carentem Sithonia nive,
　　regina, sublimi flagello
　　　tange Chloen semel arrogantem.

III.26

No problems with life,
at least from those I've loved, who testify
I've done all right

till now. So here on this mythic wall
to the left of Her shrine we've honored,
I'll hang up my old resources,

my music-making lyre, the wily crowbars, bows, torches,
all that I've used to enter
through the restricting doors.

Yet Goddess, oh Venus, who holds from the cold,
the winter's killing blast, blest Cyprus and Memphis,
one last request of You—

Please flick just once
with your imperious whip
young Chloë's disdaining bum.

Robert Creeley

III.27

Impios parrae recinentis omen
ducat et praegnas canis aut ab agro
rava decurrens lupa Lanuvino
    fetaque volpes;

rumpat et serpens iter institutum,
si per obliquum similis sagittae
terruit mannos: ego cui timebo,
    providus auspex,

antequam stantes repetat paludes
imbrium divina avis imminentum,
oscinem corvum prece suscitabo
    solis ab ortu.

sis licet felix, ubicumque mavis,
et memor nostri, Galatea, vivas;
teque nec laevus vetet ire picus
    nec vaga cornix.

sed vides, quanto trepidet tumultu
pronus Orion. ego quid sit ater
Hadriae novi sinus et quid albus
    peccet Iapyx.

hostium uxores puerique caecos
sentiant motus orientis Austri et
aequoris nigri fremitum et trementes
    verbere ripas.

sic et Europe niveum doloso
credidit tauro latus et scatentem
beluis pontum mediasque fraudes
    palluit audax.

nuper in pratis studiosa florum et
debitae Nymphis opifex coronae
nocte sublustri nihil astra praeter
    vidit et undas.

III.27

A pregnant bitch, a screech-owl with its cry
Shrill and repeated—let these terrify
The guilty wayfarer. A wolf that lopes
Across the hills, a vixen with her cubs

Or snake that like an arrow suddenly
(Frightening the horses) zips across the way—
Whole entourage of omens! I, since fear
Fills me for the travelers I hold dear,

Auspicious prophet, thus ward off all ill:
The croaking raven from the east I'll call
Before it flaps back to its marshy home
To signify the coming of a storm.

Live happily wherever you may be,
Galatea—and remember me!
Let no unlucky woodpecker or crow
Keep you from going, if you want to go.

But pay attention to how Orion sets
Amidst a storm. I know how bad it gets
On the Adriatic; how treacherously
The Northwest wind blows from a clear blue sky.

The wives and children of our enemies
Should be the ones to fear such swelling seas,
The roaring of the waters in a gale
And shores that tremble under the wind's flail.

Europa too entrusted her white shape
To the sly bull. At monsters of the deep
And perils of the open sea she quailed
And shuddered, who before had been so bold.

Expert just in flowers till yesterday,
In weaving garlands for the nymphs, now she
Could make out in the dim expanse of night
Nothing but endless waves and faint starlight.

quae simul centum tetigit potentem
oppidis Creten, "pater, o relictum
filiae nomen pietasque" dixit
   "victa furore.

unde quo veni? levis una mors est
virginum culpae. vigilansne ploro
turpe commissum an vitiis carentem
   ludit imago,

vana quae porta fugiens eburna
somnium ducit? meliusne fluctus
ire per longos fuit an recentes
   carpere flores?

si quis infamem mihi nunc iuvencum
dedat iratae, lacerare ferro et
frangere enitar modo multum amati
   cornua monstri.

impudens liqui patrios Penates,
impudens Orcum moror. o deorum
si quis haec audis, utinam inter errem
   nuda leones!

antequam turpis macies decentes
occupet malas teneraeque sucus
defluat praedae, speciosa quaero
   pascere tigris.

'vilis Europe,' pater urget absens:
'quid mori cessas? potes hac ab orno
pendulum zona bene te secuta
   laedere collum.

sive te rupes et acuta leto
saxa delectant, age te procellae
crede veloci, nisi erile mavis
   carpere pensum

232

But as soon as she reached Crete, the isle
Fabled for its hundred citadels,
"Oh father, I have madly tossed aside
A daughter's rights and duties," the girl cried.

"What place is this? One death cannot undo
The sins of guilty virgins such as me.
Am I awake—remorseful, horrified
At what I've done? Or do I sleep instead?

Did a vain image from the gate of dream
Deceive me? Did I not commit this sin?
Which should I be doing: ploughing through
Wild waves, or picking flowers fresh with dew?

Oh, if I got my hands on that bull now,
I know exactly what I'd try to do:
Snap off its horns, that monster I adored,
And stab it, penetrate it with a sword.

Oh, shameless! To abandon all I knew—
Hearth and home—and shameless to delay
Before the gates of Death. Hello? Hello?
Gods, if you hear me, naked let me go

Be food for lions! Tigers let me feed
While my flesh still is juicy, my cheeks red,
While I'm still young and beautiful to see,
Before old age and illness wither me.

'Europa'—I can hear my father now—
'What are you waiting for? Here's a handy tree;
You have your silken sash; put it to use,
Looping it into a hangman's noose.

Perhaps steep cliffs you might prefer to scale.
Sharp rocks below await you. To the gale
Launch yourself! Leap—go on—into the air!
Or would you rather, princess though you are,

regius sanguis dominaeque tradi
barbarae paelex.'" aderat querenti
perfidum ridens Venus et remisso
    filius arcu.

mox ubi lusit satis, "abstineto"
dixit "irarum calidaeque rixae,
cum tibi invisus laceranda reddet
    cornua taurus.

uxor invecti Iovis esse nescis.
mitte singultus, bene ferre magnam
disce fortunam; tua sectus orbis
    nomina ducet."

Serving as some sovereign's concubine,
Card the wool of his barbarian queen?'"
As she lamented, Venus suddenly
Appeared before her, laughing heartlessly—

Venus accompanied by her small son,
Cupid, his task complete, his bow unstrung.
Venus laughed long and loud. When she was done,
"Cool," she commanded, "this hot passion;

Calm your rage and soothe your anger's heat.
He'll soon present, this bull whom you so hate,
His horns to you for breaking. Fool! You are
(Stop sobbing, now) the wife of Jupiter,

And you must learn to bear with dignity
The burden of this mighty destiny.
Europa, yours will be unending fame;
Henceforth a continent will bear your name."

Rachel Hadas

III.28

Festo quid potius die
    Neptuni faciam? prome reconditum,
Lyde, strenua Caecubum
    munitaeque adhibe vim sapientiae.

inclinare meridiem
    sentis ac, veluti stet volucris dies,
parcis deripere horreo
    cessantem Bibuli consulis amphoram.

nos cantabimus invicem
    Neptunum et virides Nereidum comas;
tu curva recines lyra
    Latonam et celeris spicula Cynthiae;

summo carmine, quae Cnidon
    fulgentesque tenet Cycladas et Paphum
iunctis visit oloribus;
    dicetur merita Nox quoque nenia.

III.28

What could be better, on this day
    of Neptune's feast? Lyde, haul down
that old Caecubum wine, and let's
    assault the fortress of wisdom.

Already past noon, but you're delaying,
    as if the fleet hours stood still, girl;
it's waiting for us, that vintage wine
    from the years when Bibulus was consul.

We'll take turns singing. I'll do
    Neptune and the Nereid's sea-foam hair;
you, on your curving lyre, a hymn
    to Latona and the swift arrows of the moon.

And for your final song: a hymn to Venus,
    our Queen of Cnidos and the brilliant Cyclades,
drawn to Paphos by her chariot's team of swans.
    And then we'll sing a song to suit the night.

Mark Doty

III.29

Tyrrhena regum progenies, tibi
non ante verso lene merum cado
    cum flore, Maecenas, rosarum et
      pressa tuis balanus capillis

iam dudum apud me est: eripe te morae,
ne semper udum Tibur et Aefulae
    declive contempleris arvum et
      Telegoni iuga parricidae.

fastidiosam desere copiam et
molem propinquam nubibus arduis,
    omitte mirari beatae
      fumum et opes strepitumque Romae.

plerumque gratae divitibus vices
mundaeque parvo sub lare pauperum
    cenae sine aulacis et ostro
      sollicitam explicuere frontem.

iam clarus occultum Andromedae pater
ostendit ignem, iam Procyon furit
    et stella vesani Leonis
      sole dies referente siccos;

iam pastor umbras cum grege languido
rivumque fessus quaerit et horridi
    dumeta Silvani, caretque
      ripa vagis taciturna ventis.

tu civitatem quis deceat status
curas et urbi sollicitus times,
    quid Seres et regnata Cyro
      Bactra parent Tanaisque discors.

prudens futuri temporis exitum
caliginosa nocte premit deus,
    ridetque si mortalis ultra
      fas trepidat. quod adest memento

III.29

Maecenas, progeny of Tuscan kings,
My house is yours. So merely say the word:
The untouched hogshead's waiting for you there,
Crushed essences and roses for your hair.
When you go back, Tiber will still be flowing,
The sloping fields of Aefula still exist,
Tourists still swarm along those hills
Where that famous parricide took place
And is almost legendary because
It was an accident. Accept my home:
Urban fastidious plenty overfills,
High-rise bulks pollute the skies they hide—
Let go the smoke and noise, the opulence of Rome.
Change brings the rich man back to earth,
Straightforward cooking, a simple house like mine,
This sort of poverty has often soothed
The puckered forehead of despair:
No need of purple hangings, gaudy carpets there.
The Ethiop constellation threatens heat,
The rabid Dog Star roams at large, the Lion
Breathes fire against the wilting crop.
The weary shepherd with a languid flock
Seeks out the shade, the stream, the forest heart:
No promise of a breeze begins to part
This airless air or leaves the waters cool.
While you, Maecenas, study how to rule
With care, to balance probabilities,
Guess what Eastern wars impend
Or what the crafty Scythians intend.
But a wise providence wraps round in dark
All the surmised events of time to come,
And, living in our dream of happiness,
We live to rue the hurt we could not guess.
Live in the present hour and set to rights
That which asks for present thought:
Leave all the rest, you cannot dam its flow,

componere aequus; cetera fluminis
ritu feruntur, nunc medio alveo
    cum pace delabentis Etruscum
        in mare, nunc lapides adesos

stirpesque raptas et pecus et domos
volventis una non sine montium
    clamore vicinaeque silvae,
        cum fera diluvies quietos

inritat amnes. ille potens sui
laetusque deget, cui licet in diem
    dixisse "visi: cras vel atra
        nube polum pater occupato

vel sole puro; non tamen irritum,
quodcumque retro est, efficiet, neque
    diffinget infectumque reddet,
        quod fugiens semel hora vexit.

Fortuna saevo laeta negotio et
ludum insolentem ludere pertinax
    transmutat incertos honores,
        nunc mihi, nunc alii benigna.

laudo manentem; si celeres quatit
pinnas, resigno quae dedit et mea
    virtute me involvo probamque
        Pauperiem sine dote quaero.

non est meum, si mugiat Africis
malus procellis, ad miseras preces
    decurrere et votis pacisci,
        ne Cypriae Tyriaeque merces

addant avaro divitias mari:
tum me biremis praesidio scaphae
    tutum per Aegaeos tumultus
        aura feret geminusque Pollux."

A river that moves on unstoppably,
Peaceful today, tomorrow in a flood
And thronging with its echoes all the wood,
As stones, trees, flocks and houses are dragged away.
Happy the man who to himself can say
"Whatever awaits me now, I've lived today.
Let tomorrow's sky be filled
With cloud or sunshine—why should I
Discount the happiness I've had:
Fate itself cannot undo what's done
Or take away that hour's content
That came and went, yet lives within the mind.
If fortune is a woman who can find
A cruel pleasure in her occupation,
She'll still forgetfully turn kind
Veering whichever way she feels inclined.
Leaving her to her curbside station,
Let her keep the tawdry gifts she gave,
I'll live with integrity as no one's slave.
The mast that groans in storms off Africa
Is not my business: there's no need to pray
That Cyprian or Syrian merchandise
Has not pitched off the deck to feed
The wealth of the insatiable sea.
Safe aboard my two-oared skiff,
A favorable wind and I shall sail
Through whatever storms the Aegean brews
Unharmed and calm before the stiffest gale."

Charles Tomlinson

Exegi monumentum aere perennius
regalique situ pyramidum altius,
quod non imber edax, non Aquilo impotens
possit diruere aut innumerabilis
annorum series et fuga temporum.
non omnis moriar multaque pars mei
vitabit Libitinam: usque ego postera
crescam laude recens. dum Capitolium
scandet cum tacita virgine pontifex,
dicar, qua violens obstrepit Aufidus
et qua pauper aquae Daunus agrestium
regnavit populorum, ex humili potens
princeps Aeolium carmen ad Italos
deduxisse modos. sume superbiam
quaesitam meritis et mihi Delphica
lauro cinge volens, Melpomene, comam.

III.30

More enduring than bronze now is this monument
I have made, one to reach over the Pyramids'
regal heaps, one that no greedy devouring rain,
that no blustering north wind nor the run of long
years unnumbered nor ages' flight can ruin. I'll not
die entirely, some principal part of me
yet evading the great Goddess of Burials.
Evermore will I grow, quickened in later praise.
While the Pontiff shall yet climb up the Capitol,
silent Vestal beside him, they'll be saying—where
savage Aufidus roars, where in an arid land
Daunus governed his poor rustic dominion—how
it was I, though of low origins, who would first
spin Aeolian song home to Italian verse.
Take the merited, proud honors, Melpomene,
I had gained but through you, Muse, and most graciously
Place now Apollo's bays garlanded in my hair.

John Hollander

CENTENNIAL HYMN

CARMEN SAECVLARE

Phoebe silvarumque potens Diana,
lucidum caeli decus, o colendi
semper et culti, date quae precamur
    tempore sacro,

quo Sibyllini monuere versus
virgines lectas puerosque castos
dis quibus septem placuere colles
    dicere carmen.

alme Sol, curru nitido diem qui
promis et celas aliusque et idem
nasceris, possis nihil urbe Roma
    visere maius!

rite maturos aperire partus
lenis, Ilithyia, tuere matres,
sive tu Lucina probas vocari
    seu Genitalis.

diva, producas subolem patrumque
prosperes decreta super iugandis
feminis prolisque novae feraci
    lege marita,

certus undenos deciens per annos
orbis ut cantus referatque ludos
ter die claro totiensque grata
    nocte frequentes.

vosque veraces cecinisse, Parcae,
quod semel dictum stabilisque rerum
terminus servet, bona iam peractis
    iungite fata.

fertilis frugum pecorisque tellus
spicea donet Cererem corona;
nutriant fetus et aquae salubres
    et Iovis aurae.

246

CENTENNIAL HYMN

Shining Apollo, Lord of the heavens,
Diana who reigns in the deep forests' shade,
world's brightness and darkness, worshipped forever,
    hear the hymn we have made.

Now, at this time, as the Sibyl once ordered,
the best of our children, the chosen and chaste,
praise those gods who still cherish the seven, the hills
    where our city is placed.

Quickening sun-god, whose bright chariot heralds
the daylight and leads it at last to its home,
who dies and is born, anew and unchanged,
    may no town eclipse Rome!

Gracious Ilithyia, great goddess of childbirth,
protect now our mothers: whatever the name
you would go by, ever-giving Diana, Lucina,
    your power is the same:

nurture, o goddess, our children, and bless
the rites when her father hands over the bride;
make her prolific, crowd her with babies
    so that you may preside

at centuries more of such pre-ordained feast days—
at the music and games, thrice repeated in daylight
and repeated again when the westering sun
    gives way to the night.

And Fates founded of old, whose riddles speak truly,
may you continue, with each generation,
to add for us fortunate, far-reaching destinies
    to those that are gone.

Fertile and fruitful, may Earth adorn Ceres
with corn for her crown, while our flocks fill the plain;
to augment our harvests may Jove send light breezes
    and nourishing rain.

247

condito mitis placidusque telo
supplices audi pueros, Apollo;
siderum regina bicornis, audi,
    Luna, puellas.

Roma si vestrum est opus Iliaeque
litus Etruscum tenuere turmae,
iussa pars mutare Lares et urbem
    sospite cursu,

cui per ardentem sine fraude Troiam
castus Aeneas patriae superstes
liberum munivit iter, daturus
    plura relictis:

di, probos mores docili iuventae,
di, senectuti placidae quietem,
Romulae genti date remque prolemque
    et decus omne.

quaeque vos bobus veneratur albis
clarus Anchisae Venerisque sanguis,
impetret, bellante prior, iacentem
    lenis in hostem.

iam mari terraque manus potentes
Medus Albanasque timet secures,
iam Scythae responsa petunt superbi
    nuper et Indi.

iam Fides et Pax et Honor Pudorque
priscus et neglecta redire Virtus
audet, apparetque beata pleno
    copia cornu.

augur et fulgente decorus arcu
Phoebus acceptusque novem Camenis,
qui salutari levat arte fessos
    corporis artus,

Gentle Apollo, listen now to your youths
who beg for your kindness; put by your spear,
and Luna, bright star queen, incline to these girls
    who pray to you here:

if indeed Rome is yours, if that far-wandering
remnant, the refugee bands from Troy's war,
were guided to give up their gods and city
    for the Etruscan shore,

led to their liberty by noble Aeneas
who outlived his land, whom Troy's fire laid no hand on,
who was fated to bring them in time far more
    than they would abandon,

then, o gods, make our young men tractable
and virtuous; to our old, grant peaceful health,
give to the whole race of Romulus glory,
    descendants and wealth.

Now, through us, the son of Anchises and Venus,
with these white heifers' sacrifice, will entreat
victory over our enemies, and mercy
    to those we defeat:

now our Alban axes and our gathering forces
terrify the Parthians, on land and at sea,
and those once proud peoples, the Indians and Scythians,
    await our decree;

now Faith and Peace, ancient Probity, Honor,
neglected Virtue, return; and Plenty shows
her loveliest face once more in our midst, as
    her horn overflows.

And Phoebus Apollo, in his wisdom—loved
by the nine muses, glorious with his shining bow,
who heals by his skills all the sufferings with which
    the body's laid low,

si Palatinas videt aequus aras,
remque Romanam Latiumque felix
alterum in lustrum meliusque semper
    proroget aevum,

quaeque Aventinum tenet Algidumque,
quindecim Diana preces virorum
curet et votis puerorum amicas
    applicet aures.

haec Iovem sentire deosque cunctos
spem bonam certamque domum reporto
doctus et Phoebi chorus et Dianae
    dicere laudes.

if he looks on our altars raised on the Palatine
with any approbation—may he further our endeavor,
widening, improving our power and prosperity
　　for ever and ever:

and so too may Diana, to whom the Aventine slopes,
and the Latian, are sacred, consider with care
the petition of our fifteen elders; may she grant
　　our children's prayer.

So we turn home, trusting Jove and the gods
approve our petition, that their favor will follow—
we, the chorus, who have been trained in the praise
　　of Diana, Apollo.

Dick Davis

LIBER | BOOK IV

IV. 1

Intermissa, Venus, diu
    rursus bella moves. parce, precor, precor.
non sum qualis eram bonae
    sub regno Cinarae. desine, dulcium

mater saeva Cupidinum,
    circa lustra decem flectere mollibus
iam durum imperiis: abi,
    quo blandae iuvenum te revocant preces.

tempestivius in domum
    Pauli, purpureis ales oloribus,
comissabere Maximi,
    si torrere iecur quaeris idoneum.

namque et nobilis et decens
    et pro sollicitis non tacitus reis
et centum puer artium
    late signa feret militiae tuae;

et quandoque potentior
    largi muneribus riserit aemuli,
Albanos prope te lacus
    ponet marmoream sub trabe citrea.

illic plurima naribus
    duces tura lyraeque et Berecyntiae
delectabere tibiae
    mixtis carminibus non sine fistula;

illic bis pueri die
    numen cum teneris virginibus tuum
laudantes pede candido
    in morem Salium ter quatient humum.

IV. 1

So it's war again, Venus,
after all this time? Spare me, for Goddess' sake!
    I'm not what I used to be
in dear Cynara's days, or nights. Merciless Mother
    of immoderate cravings,
fifty years have made me callous to your soft
    commands. Try elsewhere, answer
some young man's eager prayers, drive your silver swans
    to Paulus Maximus's house,
for instance—that's the right address for some fun.
    He's handsome and high-minded,
always happy to speak in behalf of the helpless;
    he's the man with the talents
to carry your banner in triumph wherever
    triumph carries *him!* And once
he's duly vanquished some squandering rival,
    he'll be likely to erect
under a cedar arbor, near Lake Alba,
    a marble statue to you,
and there inhaling sweet clouds of incense,
    and listening to music
of flutes and lyres and Berecyntian horns,
    you will be pleased to be praised
twice daily by boys and tender girls dancing
    in your honor, shining feet
stamping in the triple-time Salian mode.

me nec femina nec puer
    iam nec spes animi credula mutui
nec certare iuvat mero
    nec vincire novis tempora floribus.

sed cur heu, Ligurine, cur
    manat rara meas lacrima per genas?
cur facunda parum decoro
    inter verba cadit lingua silentio?

nocturnis ego somniis
    iam captum teneo, iam volucrem sequor
te per gramina Martii
    Campi, te per aquas, dure, volubilis.

Myself, I have no use for
tender girls, or boys either, have abandoned
    all hope of love's return; wine
leaves me cold, and garlands only make me sneeze . . .
    Then why, Ligurinus, why
do my eyes sometimes fill, even spill over?
    Why, sometimes, when I'm talking
do I suddenly have nothing to say? Why
    do I hold you in my arms
in certain dreams, certain nights, and in others
    chase you endlessly across
the Field of Mars, into the swirling Tiber?

Richard Howard

IV. 2

Pindarum quisquis studet aemulari,
Iule, ceratis ope Daedalea
nititur pinnis vitreo daturus
    nomina ponto.

monte decurrens velut amnis, imbres
quem super notas aluere ripas,
fervet immensusque ruit profundo
    Pindarus ore,

laurea donandus Apollinari,
seu per audaces nova dithyrambos
verba devolvit numerisque fertur
    lege solutis,

seu deos regesque canit, deorum
sanguinem, per quos cecidere iusta
morte Centauri, cecidit tremendae
    flamma Chimaerae,

sive quos Elea domum reducit
palma caelestes pugilemve equumve
dicit et centum potiore signis
    munere donat,

flebili sponsae iuvenemve raptum
plorat et vires animumque moresque
aureos educit in astra nigroque
    invidet Orco.

multa Dircaeum levat aura cycnum,
tendit, Antoni, quotiens in altos
nubium tractus. ego apis Matinae
    more modoque

grata carpentis thyma per laborem
plurimum circa nemus uvidique
Tiburis ripas operosa parvus
    carmina fingo.

IV.2

A poet aspiring to write Pindarically
Needs wings of wax such as Daedalus made. His fame,
When he splashes like Icarus into some shining sea,
Will lie in the body of water bearing his name.

Pindar, like a rapid mountain stream
Bursting its banks after torrential rain,
Boiling, seething, rushes on full steam
Ahead. His voice is a rich baritone,

Worthy of laurels from the god of song
Whether through daring dithyrambs he rolls
Brand-new words majestically along,
Disregarding meter's petty rules,

Whether his theme is gods or heroes—kings
Of seed divine—through whom the Centaurs came
To their deserved end (he also sings
The quenching of the dire Chimera's flame),

Or whether he tunes his instrument to extol
Olympic victories—boxing, racing, all
The ways returning victors can excel—
Odes worth a hundred statues in a hall,

Dumb on their pedestals. Or he mourns the loss
Of a young husband dead before his time,
Praises his virtues and consoles his spouse,
Condemning all of Hades' shadowy realm.

This Theban swan, Antonius, seems to rise
Each time he sings, as if a helpful breeze
Held him up until he reached the skies.
A breeze? A gale. My style is like the bees

That gather patiently from here and there
Pollen (in the woods and on both sides
Of the Tiber, thyme perfumes the air);
Humbly I shape my careful little odes.

concines maiore poeta plectro
Caesarem, quandoque trahet feroces
per sacrum clivum merita decorus
    fronde Sygambros;

quo nihil maius meliusve terris
fata donavere bonique divi,
nec dabunt, quamvis redeant in aurum
    tempora priscum.

concines laetosque dies et urbis
publicum ludum super impetrato
fortis Augusti reditu forumque
    litibus orbum.

tum meae, siquid loquar audiendum,
vocis accedet bona pars, et "O sol
pulcher, o laudande!" canam recepto
    Caesare felix.

tuque dum procedis, io Triumphe!
non semel dicemus, "io Triumphe!"
civitas omnis dabimusque divis
    tura benignis.

te decem tauri totidemque vaccae,
me tener solvet vitulus, relicta
matre qui largis iuvenescit herbis
    in mea vota,

fronte curvatos imitatus ignis
tertium lunae referentis ortum,
qua notam duxit, niveus videri,
    cetera fulvus.

You, at another level of ambition,
Shall sing of Caesar when, triumphantly
Leading savage tribes in a procession
Along the Sacred Way, he's rightfully

Crowned with a garland. Caesar, best of men
(How could the fates and gods improve on him?)
We have been graced with or will be again,
Even if we could somehow turn back time

To the Golden Age. Among your themes
Of song will be feast days in celebration
Of Caesar's safe return; and public games;
And the Forum finally free of litigation.

And only then, if I have anything
To say worth hearing, will I raise my voice.
"Oh glorious praiseworthy day!" I'll sing,
Happy that Caesar is restored to us.

You lead the way. "Oh triumph!" we will cry.
"Triumph! Triumph!" not just once or twice
But all together and repeatedly,
Then to the kind gods offer frankincense.

Bulls and cows, ten of each—this was your vow.
Only one tender little calf is mine,
Recently weaned, and starting now to grow
Strong as it grazes happily in green

Meadows. Its forehead imitates the bright
Curving contours of a crescent moon;
Its markings, where it has them, snowy white,
The rest all a soft brown.

Rachel Hadas

Quem tu, Melpomene, semel
   nascentem placido lumine videris,
illum non labor Isthmius
   clarabit pugilem, non equus impiger

curru ducet Achaico
   victorem, neque res bellica Deliis
ornatum foliis ducem,
   quod regum tumidas contuderit minas,

ostendet Capitolio;
   sed quae Tibur aquae fertile praefluunt
et spissae nemorum comae
   fingent Aeolio carmine nobilem.

Romae principis urbium
   dignatur suboles inter amabiles
vatum ponere me choros,
   et iam dente minus mordeor invido.

o testudinis aureae
   dulcem quae strepitum, Pieri, temperas,
o mutis quoque piscibus
   donatura cycni, si libeat, sonum,

totum muneris hoc tui est,
   quod monstror digito praetereuntium
Romanae fidicen lyrae:
   quod spiro et placeo, si placeo, tuum est.

IV.3

Whom once, Melpomene, you gazed upon
  With kindly favor at his birth,
Is not fated to be, say, a famous boxer;
  No impetuous stallion will pull his chariot

First to the finish line, no feats of war
  Escort him in triumph to the Capitol,
A hero crowned with laurel for having crushed
  The haughty threats of foreign kings.

Instead, the waters flowing past the rich fields
  And shady groves of Tibur's green retreats
Will hear his sweet Aeolian songs
  And carry downstream his fame.

By the people of Rome, the queen of cities,
  I have been chosen as worthy of a place
Among the noble choirs of her lyric poets,
  And already I feel beyond the reach of envy.

O Pierian muse, you who modulates the delicate
  Harmonies of the lyre's golden form,
O you who could, if you wished, bestow
  The song of swans on silent fish,

This is your gift to me, that I am pointed out
  By passersby as the poet of Rome,
That the pleasure of my poems, if they please,
  Is your pleasure, your inspiration.

                    J. D. McClatchy

IV.4

Qualem ministrum fulminis alitem,
cui rex deorum regnum in aves vagas
   permisit expertus fidelem
     Iuppiter in Ganymede flavo,

olim iuventas et patrius vigor
nido laborum propulit inscium,
   vernique iam nimbis remotis
     insolitos docuere nisus

venti paventem, mox in ovilia
demisit hostem vividus impetus,
   nunc in reluctantes dracones
     egit amor dapis atque pugnae;

qualemve laetis caprea pascuis
intenta fulvae matris ab ubere
   iam lacte depulsum leonem
     dente novo peritura vidit:

videre Raetis bella sub Alpibus
Drusum gerentem Vindelici; (quibus
   mos unde deductus per omne
     tempus Amazonia securi

dextras obarmet, quaerere distuli,
nec scire fas est omnia) sed diu
   lateque victrices catervae
     consiliis iuvenis revictae

IV.4

Like the winged brandisher
of lightning (Mercury, to whom
Jupiter, king of the gods, gave
power over the birdlike winds, after

finding him loyal in the affair
of blond Ganymede), at first
youth and a strength inherited have
driven him, a stranger as yet

to suffering, from the nest; then
the spring winds—all clouds gone—
schooled him, though afraid,
in the kind of toiling he'd known

nothing of; soon enough, a force
all but palpable has sent him
as enemy to the sheepfolds, a love
of plunder and battle itself drives him

against the snakes' wrestlings;
or like—just weaned from the breast
of its tawny mother—that lion
which the roe-deer, soon to perish, catches

sight of in the lush of meadow;
so did Drusus, waging war
beneath the Raetian Alps, seem
to the Vindelici—about whose

custom of always wielding
the Amazonian ax in the right hand
I make no speculation;
it isn't right to know everything.

But those troops whose victory had been
so extensive, for so long,
found themselves again
conquered—this time by the wiles

sensere quid mens, rite quid indoles
nutrita faustis sub penetralibus
   posset, quid Augusti paternus
      in pueros animus Nerones.

fortes creantur fortibus et bonis;
est in iuvencis, est in equis patrum
   virtus, neque imbellem feroces
      progenerant aquilae columbam.

doctrina sed vim promovet insitam,
rectique cultus pectora roborant;
   utcumque defecere mores,
      indecorant bene nata culpae.

quid debeas, o Roma, Neronibus,
testis Metaurum flumen et Hasdrubal
   devictus et pulcher fugatis
      ille dies Latio tenebris,

qui primus alma risit adorea,
dirus per urbes Afer ut Italas
   ceu flamma per taedas vel Eurus
      per Siculas equitavit undas.

of youth: they learned the capabilities
of a properly nourished mind, of sheer
character when reared in a home
the gods favor,

and of the paternal spirit of Augustus
toward the young Neros.
From the strong and the good,
the strong are made;

to cattle, to horses also,
a glory inherited from the fathers.
Fierce eagles do not sire
the fightless dove. No:

discipline brings out inherent
strength, and correct training
makes firm the spirit;
wherever morals are scant, the flaw

ruins even the well-born.
Rome,
what you owe to the Neros
the Metaurus River is witness to,

as is Hasdrubal in his defeat;
also that lovely day when, all
shadow having been put at last
to flight from Latium, nourishing

glory smiled for the first time
since the fierce African galloped
through the Italian cities,
as a flame through pines,

post hoc secundis usque laboribus
Romana pubes crevit, et impio
   vastata Poenorum tumultu
      fana deos habuere rectos.

dixitque tandem perfidus Hannibal:
"cervi luporum praeda rapacium,
   sectamur ultro, quos opimus
      fallere et effugere est triumphus.

gens, quae cremato fortis ab Ilio
iactata Tuscis aequoribus sacra
   natosque maturosque patres
      pertulit Ausonias ad urbes,

duris ut ilex tonsa bipennibus
nigrae feraci frondis in Algido,
   per damna, per caedes ab ipso
      ducit opes animumque ferro.

non hydra secto corpore firmior
vinci dolentem crevit in Herculem,
   monstrumve submisere Colchi
      maius Echioniaeve Thebae.

as across Sicilian waters
the East wind.
After this, their labors
successful, the Roman youth flourished,

and the shrines once gutted by
the impious Punic mob held
again their gods in place,
and at last the faithless Hannibal said:

"As deer, the plunder of violent wolves,
we follow those whom it was our
especial triumph, once, to deceive
and put to rout.

The race that was strong even when
tossed from fire-ruined Troy
over the Tuscan seas, the race that
brought its sacred relics, its people

young and old to the cities of Ausonia,
now like an ilex—shorn
by the harsh ax on Mount Algidos, thick
with black leafage—through loss, through

slaughter, from the iron itself it draws
both wealth and power.
The hydra, its body in pieces,
did not rise stronger against some

aching-with-defeat Hercules,
nor did the Colchians or Echionian
Thebes send forward any greater
monster. Sink it into the depths,

merses profundo, pulchrior evenit;
luctere, multa proruet integrum
   cum laude victorem geretque
      proelia coniugibus loquenda.

Carthagini iam non ego nuntios
mittam superbos: occidit, occidit
   spes omnis et fortuna nostri
      nominis Hasdrubale interempto.

nil Claudiae non perficient manus,
quas et benigno numine Iuppiter
   defendit et curae sagaces
      expediunt per acuta belli."

it emerges more beautiful;
wrestle it, it rushes unharmed
against its conqueror,
to its own praise, waging

battles for wives to tell of.
No longer shall I send to Carthage
my boastful reports:
lost, all hope

is lost, along with the fortune
that our name once was, now
Hasdrubal is destroyed.
Nothing is unattainable

for the Claudians, whom Jupiter defends
with kindly power—
whom shrewd counsels help
negotiate the harshnesses of war."

Carl Phillips

Divis orte bonis, optime Romulae
custos gentis, abes iam nimium diu;
maturum reditum pollicitus patrum
    sancto concilio redi.

lucem redde tuae, dux bone, patriae:
instar veris enim vultus ubi tuus
adfulsit populo, gratior it dies
    et soles melius nitent.

ut mater iuvenem, quem Notus invido
flatu Carpathii trans maris aequora
cunctantem spatio longius annuo
    dulci distinet a domo,

votis ominibusque et precibus vocat,
curvo nec faciem litore demovet:
sic desideriis icta fidelibus
    quaerit patria Caesarem.

tutus bos etenim rura perambulat,
nutrit rura Ceres almaque Faustitas,
pacatum volitant per mare navitae;
    culpari metuit fides,

nullis polluitur casta domus stupris,
mos et lex maculosum edomuit nefas,
laudantur simili prole puerperae,
    culpam poena premit comes.

quis Parthum paveat, quis gelidum Scythen,
quis Germania quos horrida parturit
fetus, incolumi Caesare? quis ferae
    bellum curet Hiberiae?

IV.5

Born of heavenly gods, peerless guardian
of the tribe of Romulus, your absence has been
too long. Return quickly, just as you promised
    the sacred council of fathers.

Blessed leader, restore the light of our country,
for when like spring your image warms
the people, the day passes more pleasantly,
    and the sun shines more brilliantly.

Just as a mother pines for her young son—
kept away for more than a year by jealous winds,
beyond the calm waters of the Carpathian sea,
    from his sweet and temperate home—

making vows, consulting omens, saying prayers,
and keeping her eyes fixed on the curving shores,
this country, stricken by loyalty, yearns
    for the quick return of Caesar.

For when he is here, cattle wander the fields safely,
Ceres and Prosperity nourish the family farm,
ships sail swiftly through peaceful seas,
    Virtue is wary of censure.

Decent houses are not soiled or violated,
morality and law conquer foul crime,
wives give birth to children that resemble husbands,
    Punishment consumes the guilty.

Who would fear the Parthians, who the cold
Scythians, who the swarming brood of Germany,
while Caesar is safe? Who would care about
    war in savage Iberia?

condit quisque diem collibus in suis,
et vitem viduas ducit ad arbores;
hinc ad vina redit laetus et alteris
    te mensis adhibet deum;

te multa prece, te prosequitur mero
defuso pateris, et Laribus tuum
miscet numen, uti Graecia Castoris
    et magni memor Herculis.

"longas o utinam, dux bone, ferias
praestes Hesperiae!" dicimus integro
sicci mane die, dicimus uvidi,
    cum sol Oceano subest.

On his hill, each man spends the day marrying
vines to widowed trees, then goes jubilantly
to take his wine, and at the second course
    calls upon your divinity.

You he pursues with prayers, and to you dedicates
libations of wine, mixing your divine heritage
with his household gods, as Greece remembers
    Castor and mighty Hercules.

"Oh, blessed leader, please bestow a long peace
on Hesperia!" we pray for your authority
when we are dry at daybreak and wine-drenched
    as the sun enters the Ocean.

John Kinsella

IV.6

Dive, quem proles Niobea magnae
vindicem linguae Tityosque raptor
sensit et Troiae prope victor altae
   Phthius Achilles,

ceteris maior, tibi miles impar,
filius quamvis Thetidis marinae
Dardanas turres quateret tremenda
   cuspide pugnax.

ille, mordaci velut icta ferro
pinus aut impulsa cupressus Euro,
procidit late posuitque collum in
   pulvere Teucro.

ille non inclusus equo Minervae
sacra mentito male feriatos
Troas et laetam Priami choreis
   falleret aulam;

sed palam captis gravis, heu nefas, heu,
nescios fari pueros Achivis
ureret flammis, etiam latentem
   matris in alvo,

ni tuis victus Venerisque gratae
vocibus divom pater adnuisset
rebus Aeneae potiore ductos
   alite muros.

doctor argutae fidicen Thaliae,
Phoebe, qui Xantho lavis amne crinis,
Dauniae defende decus Camenae,
   levis Agyieu.

IV.6

Apollo, whom Niobe's children would come to know as the scourge
of braggarts and blowhards, whom Tityos the wide-boy
would come to know, as would Achilles of Phthia, on the verge
of taking the ramparts of Troy,

peerless-in-battle Achilles who met his peer
in you, despite his being the son of a sea goddess, Thetis, despite
his having rattled with his spear
those same ramparts of Troy, Achilles of such might

who would nonetheless fall
headlong like a pine before a curt
edge of steel, or a cypress toppled by a sudden squall
from the east, lying flat on his face in the dirt,

Achilles who would never stoop
to skulking within a horse made of wood,
that fake offering to Minerva, or dupe
the Trojans into doomed dancing, their fatal festive mood,

but would quite barefacedly have sent prisoners-of-war to meet their fate,
quite brazenly sent to their doom
with blastings and burnings—horrific to relate—
not only babes-in-arms but infants in the womb,

had not the father of the gods,
in response to your own and Venus's calls,
given the nod
and assigned to Aeneas the plan of some rather more auspicious city
    walls—

would that you who taught Thalia herself the lyre,
you who wash your hair in the Xanthus, you smooth-shaven
smoother of the ways, would that you might grant the Muse who inspires
the poets of Apulia safe haven,

spiritum Phoebus mihi, Phoebus artem
carminis nomenque dedit poetae.
virginum primae puerique claris
    patribus orti,

Deliae tutela deae, fugacis
lyncas et cervos cohibentis arcu,
Lesbium servate pedem meique
    pollicis ictum,

rite Latonae puerum canentes,
rite crescentem face Noctilucam,
prosperam frugum celeremque pronos
    volvere menses.

nupta iam dices "ego dis amicum,
saeculo festas referente luces,
reddidi carmen docilis modorum
    vatis Horati."

having already blown on my poetic ember
and allowed the poetic flame to blaze in me.
And now, all of you chorus members,
all of you sons and daughters of the noblest pedigree,

all of you in the care of Diana, Diana on whose arrows the fleet
lynxes and deer always come
to grief, try to keep the beat
and follow the stroke on the lyre of my thumb

as you sing a song
of praise to the selfsame moon goddess whose torch burns
more strongly even as she makes the crops grow strong
and the months of the year turn.

One day, when you're married, you'll say,
"I sang the responses, when the time rolled round for us
to perform the Hundred Year Hymn for the gods, I who'd been instructed
      in the ways
of the poet, Horace."

Paul Muldoon

IV.7

Diffugere nives, redeunt iam gramina campis
    arboribusque comae;
mutat terra vices et decrescentia ripas
    flumina praetereunt;

Gratia cum Nymphis geminisque sororibus audet
    ducere nuda choros.
immortalia ne speres, monet annus et almum
    quae rapit hora diem.

frigora mitescunt zephyris, ver proterit aestas
    interitura simul
pomifer autumnus fruges effuderit, et mox
    bruma recurrit iners.

damna tamen celeres reparant caelestia lunae;
    nos ubi decidimus,
quo pius Aeneas, quo Tullus dives et Ancus,
    pulvis et umbra sumus.

quis scit an adiciant hodiernae crastina summae
    tempora di superi?
cuncta manus avidas fugient heredis, amico
    quae dederis animo.

cum semel occideris et de te splendida Minos
    fecerit arbitria,
non, Torquate, genus, non te facundia, non te
    restituet pietas;

infernis neque enim tenebris Diana pudicum
    liberat Hippolytum,
nec Lethaea valet Theseus abrumpere caro
    vincula Pirithoo.

IV.7

All gone, the snow: grass throngs back to the fields,
the trees grow out new hair;
earth follows her changes, and subsiding streams
jostle within their banks.

The three graces and the greenwood nymphs,
naked, dare to dance.
You won't live always, warn the year and the hour,
seizing the honeyed day.

Cold softens in breezes, spring fades into summer's heat
no sooner felt than doomed
when autumn pours out its harvest fruits, and soon
ice-solid winter steps back.

Swift-changing moons repair these heavenly hurts.
But we, when we go down
where pious Aeneas, rich Tullus, and Ancus have gone,
we're nothing but dust and shade.

Who knows how many tomorrows the gods will add
to today's small sum?
Whatever you spend in pleasures now, you won't
leave in your heir's moist grip.

Once you've died, and Minos has passed his mighty
sentence on you, Torquatus,
not family name, nor virtue, nor ingenious speeches will ever
spirit you back to life.

Not even Diana frees chaste Hippolytus
from the Underworld dark;
and Theseus hasn't the strength to loosen death's chains
from Pirithous, whom he loved.

Rosanna Warren

Donarem pateras grataque commodus,
Censorine, meis aera sodalibus,
donarem tripodas, praemia fortium
Graiorum, neque tu pessima munerum
ferres, divite me scilicet artium,
quas aut Parrhasius protulit aut Scopas,
hic saxo, liquidis ille coloribus
sollers nunc hominem ponere, nunc deum.
sed non haec mihi vis, non tibi talium
res est aut animus deliciarum egens.
gaudes carminibus: carmina possumus
donare et pretium dicere muneri.
non incisa notis marmora publicis,
per quae spiritus et vita redit bonis
post mortem ducibus, non celeres fugae
reiectaeque retrorsum Hannibalis minae,
non incendia Carthaginis impiae
eius, qui domita nomen ab Africa
lucratus rediit, clarius indicant
laudes quam Calabrae Pierides neque,
si chartae sileant quod bene feceris,
mercedem tuleris. quid foret Iliae
Mavortisque puer, si taciturnitas
obstaret meritis invida Romuli?
ereptum Stygiis fluctibus Aeacum
virtus et favor et lingua potentium
vatum divitibus consecrat insulis.
dignum laude virum Musa vetat mori.
caelo Musa beat. sic Iovis interest
optatis epulis impiger Hercules,
clarum Tyndaridae sidus ab infimis
quassas eripiunt aequoribus rates,
ornatus viridi tempora pampino
Liber vota bonos ducit ad exitus.

IV.8

If I could afford to, I'd shower all my friends
with gifts, with bronzes and bowls and tripods
like the prizes of brawny Greeks, and you, Censorinus,
would have the best of them, the most skillfully sculpted
marble gods of Parrhasius or the watercolor heroes
of Scopas. But I can't offer such tangible trifles.
I know what you want from me: the even more
delightful tribute of songs. I can give you songs,
and both of us know their value. No marble carved
with facts can bring heroes back to life. Only the Muse
could record the swift retreat of Hannibal
and pour his deadly threats back into his mouth
and keep terrible Carthage burning forever
and preserve the fame of him who returned home
with a name that meant the defeat of Africa.
You wouldn't profit at all from your great deeds
if no poet told the tale. What would the son of Mars
and Ilia be if envy had kept the Muse
from singing aloud the praises of Romulus?
The voices of great poets and their good opinions
have hauled Aeacus, dripping, out of the Styx
and made him immortal in the Blessed Isles.
Poets won't let praiseworthy men die.
Poets lift them to heaven. Castor and Pollux
burn in the night sky because of us
And rescue ships in peril, and Hercules
himself is feasting with Jove because we said so,
and Bacchus, with vine tendrils curled at his ears,
because of us, grants you your anxious prayers.

David Wagoner

IV. 9

Ne forte credas interitura quae
longe sonantem natus ad Aufidum
    non ante vulgatas per artes
        verba loquor socianda chordis:

non, si priores Maeonius tenet
sedes Homerus, Pindaricae latent
    Ceaeque et Alcaei minaces
        Stesichorique graves Camenae;

nec siquid olim lusit Anacreon
delevit aetas; spirat adhuc amor
    vivuntque commissi calores
        Aeoliae fidibus puellae.

non sola comptos arsit adulteri
crines et aurum vestibus illitum
    mirata regalesque cultus
        et comites Helene Lacaena,

primusve Teucer tela Cydonio
direxit arcu; non semel Ilios
    vexata; non pugnavit ingens
        Idomeneus Sthenelusve solus

dicenda Musis proelia; non ferox
Hector vel acer Deiphobus graves
    excepit ictus pro pudicis
        coniugibus puerisque primus.

vixere fortes ante Agamemnona
multi; sed omnes inlacrimabiles
    urgentur ignotique longa
        nocte, carent quia vate sacro.

It never should be thought that the words will die
which I, born near far-echoing Aufidus,
    ally now with the lyre in modes that
        never before have been too familiar.

Maeonian Homer holds the most honored place,
Though Pindar's Muse has not been obscured, nor tough
    Alcaeus', Simonides',
        that of the stately Stesichorus; nor

has time undone Anacreon's playful stuff,
and Sappho's love keeps breathing away: the heat
    of all that passion still survives which
        once she entrusted her instrument with.

Not only Sparta's Helen became inflamed
with love, admiring his carefully managed hair,
    his gold-bespangled clothes, his princely
        bearing and entourage there behind him;

the first to send a shaft from a Cretan bow
was hardly Teucer; Troy under siege was not
    unique; the huge Idomeneus,
        Sthenelus—neither alone fought battles

deserving Muses' song; nor were Hector, brave
in fighting, nor the mighty Deiphobus
    the very first to take such heavy
        blows for their virtuous wives and children.

There lived before Agamemnon multitudes
of heroes, driven down into endless night,
    unknown and unlamented, wanting
        praise of the consecrated poet.

paulum sepultae distat inertiae
celata virtus. non ego te meis
   chartis inornatum silebo,
      totve tuos patiar labores

impune, Lolli, carpere lividas
obliviones. est animus tibi
   rerumque prudens et secundis
      temporibus dubiisque rectus,

vindex avarae fraudis et abstinens
ducentis ad se cuncta pecuniae,
   consulque non unius anni,
      sed quotiens bonus atque fidus

iudex honestum praetulit utili,
reiecit alto dona nocentium
   vultu, per obstantes catervas
      explicuit sua victor arma.

non possidentem multa vocaveris
recte beatum; rectius occupat
   nomen beati, qui deorum
      muneribus sapienter uti

duramque callet pauperiem pati
peiusque leto flagitium timet,
   non ille pro caris amicis
      aut patria timidus perire.

Within the tomb there's little that separates
a hidden worthiness from inertia. You
   will never stay uncelebrated,
      Lollius, here in my poems, nor will I

let envious oblivion pluck apart
all your many labors. You have a mind
   experienced and forward-looking,
      steady throughout the shifts of fortune;

you punish greedy fraudulence, keeping far
from money drawing everything to itself,
   you, consul not of just one year but
      often, a judge who is good and true, you

prefer the honest to the expedient,
with high disdain rejecting the bribes that guilt
   will offer, carrying your arms in
      victory through the opposing forces.

Of men of wealth it cannot be rightly said
that he was ever truly a happy one,
   but he more rightly claims that name who
      knows how to use what the gods have given,

who knows the hardest poverty and endures
it, he who fears dishonor far more than death
   and who is unafraid to die for
      dearest of friends or beloved country.

John Hollander

IV. 10

O crudelis adhuc et Veneris muneribus potens,
insperata tuae cum veniet pluma superbiae
et, quae nunc umeris involitant, deciderint comae,
nunc et qui color est puniceae flore prior rosae
mutatus, Ligurine, in faciem verterit hispidam:
dices "heu," quotiens te speculo videris alterum,
"quae mens est hodie, cur eadem non puero fuit,
vel cur his animis incolumes non redeunt genae?"

Cocksure and licensed so by Venus' gifts,
what'll you say to your glass, Ligurinus,
when "feathers" first poke through unbroken cheeks,
when a perfect complexion shows . . . imperfections
and curls once falling to your shoulders have . . . fallen?
That boy can't fathom today's experience;
yesterday's flesh can't furbish this strange man.
"I am," you'll say, "no longer one and the same."

Richard Howard

Est mihi nonum superantis annum
plenus Albani cadus; est in horto,
Phylli, nectendis apium coronis;
    est hederae vis

multa, qua crines religata fulges;
ridet argento domus; ara castis
vincta verbenis avet immolato
    spargier agno;

cuncta festinat manus, huc et illuc
cursitant mixtae pueris puellae;
sordidum flammae trepidant rotantes
    vertice fumum.

ut tamen noris quibus advoceris
gaudiis, Idus tibi sunt agendae,
qui dies mensem Veneris marinae
    findit Aprilem,

iure sollemnis mihi sanctiorque
paene natali proprio, quod ex hac
luce Maecenas meus adfluentes
    ordinat annos.

Telephum, quem tu petis, occupavit
non tuae sortis iuvenem puella
dives et lasciva tenetque grata
    compede vinctum.

terret ambustus Phaëthon avaras
spes, et exemplum grave praebet ales
Pegasus terrenum equitem gravatus
    Bellerophontem,

IV.11

Phyllis, I've saved a flagon brimmed with wine
nine years old, from the hills of Alba.
In the garden is parsley to weave into garlands
    and ivy to bind back your hair

and illuminate your beauty again. In the villa,
the best silver is polished and shining,
the altar strewn with laurel that anticipates
    the blood of a sacrificed lamb.

Everyone hurries to make the house ready;
the servants bustle, boys and girls together,
and resplendent fires send up columns of smoke
    that rise to make a wreath.

Let me tell you: We celebrate this day, the Ides
of Venus's April, as a day of festival, very nearly
as festive as my own birthday, for it is the day
    by which Maecenas counts his years.

Phyllis, give up your yearning for Telephus,
born so far above you, in love with a rich
and lusty girl who keeps him bound
    in chains of sensual pleasure.

Let Phaëthon be a warning to you—
burned because his desire reached too high.
Pegasus the winged horse could not
    fly and still carry Bellerophon.

Limit yourself to what's possible, Phyllis.
Don't waste yourself desiring something
you cannot possess—the misfortune
    of yearning for a man

semper ut te digna sequare et ultra
quam licet sperare nefas putando
disparem vites. age iam, meorum
    finis amorum,

(non enim posthae alia calebo
femina) condisce modos, amanda
voce quos reddas: minuentur atrae
    carmine curae.

who's unattainable. Phyllis, listen to me.
You are the last of my loves. I will never
desire or pursue another woman.
    Come and sing for me now

in your voice as beautiful as you are.
Singing a new song will help you dismiss
your disappointment over your love,
    and a song will lighten your heart.

Donald Hall

Iam veris comites, quae mare temperant,
impellunt animae lintea Thraciae;
iam nec prata rigent nec fluvii strepunt
   hiberna nive turgidi.

nidum ponit, Ityn flebiliter gemens,
infelix avis et Cecropiae domus
aeternum opprobrium, quod male barbaras
   regum est ulta libidines.

dicunt in tenero gramine pinguium
custodes ovium carmina fistula
delectantque deum, cui pecus et nigri
   colles Arcadiae placent.

adduxere sitim tempora, Vergili;
sed pressum Calibus ducere Liberum
si gestis, iuvenum nobilium cliens,
   nardo vina merebere.

nardi parvus onyx eliciet cadum,
qui nunc Sulpiciis adcubat horreis,
spes donare novas largus amaraque
   curarum eluere efficax.

ad quae si properas gaudia, cum tua
velox merce veni: non ego te meis
immunem meditor tingere poculis,
   plena dives ut in domo.

verum pone moras et studium lucri
nigrorumque memor, dum licet, ignium
misce stultitiam consiliis brevem;
   dulce est desipere in loco.

IV. 12

Already the winds of Thrace, spring's attendant ecstasy,
Damp down the waves and the sea and swell the sails,
Meadows shrink back in thaw, rivers quieten their moan,
Lacking the winter's melt.

The swallow comes back and builds her nest again,
Unfortunate bird, still grieving for luckless Itys,
Still bearing the endless shame of over-vengefulness
On her sadistic and lustful king.

Shepherds laze in the new grass and tend their sheep,
Playing their pipes and singing, delighting the great god Pan
To whom all flocks are dear that browse
The shadowy, green hills of Arcadia.

A season, in short, Virgilius, that raises a thirst;
But if you want a well-aged, robust Calenian wine,
Then you, my courtier friend, must pay your way
With equal value in oil of spikenard.

One onyx box of spikenard will buy us that jar of wine
From those in stock in the warehouse of Sulpicius,
A big wine that will expand the heart and work
Its wonders to wash your bitter cares away.

If such diversion entices you, come on
And bring the merchandise; but don't come empty-handed,
As I'm not running a handout wet bar
The way your patrician friends so often do.

Seriously, now, put off all thought of cost and dallying,
Remember death's dark burning, and while there's still time,
Mix up your wise ways with a bit of folly;
A little foolishness is sometimes sweet.

Charles Wright

IV. 13

Audivere, Lyce, di mea vota, di
audivere, Lyce: fis anus et tamen
　　vis formosa videri
　　　　ludisque et bibis impudens

et cantu tremulo pota Cupidinem
lentum sollicitas. ille virentis et
　　doctae psallere Chiae
　　　　pulchris excubat in genis.

importunus enim transvolat aridas
quercus, et refugit te, quia luridi
　　dentes te, quia rugae
　　　　turpant et capitis nives.

nec Coae referunt iam tibi purpurae
nec cari lapides tempora, quae semel
　　notis condita fastis
　　　　inclusit volucris dies.

quo fugit Venus, heu, quove color? decens
quo motus? quid habes illius, illius,
　　quae spirabat amores,
　　　　quae me surpuerat mihi,

felix post Cinaram notaque et artium
gratarum facies? sed Cinarae breves
　　annos Fata dederunt,
　　　　servatura diu parem

cornicis vetulae temporibus Lycen,
possent ut iuvenes visere fervidi
　　multo non sine risu
　　　　dilapsam in cineres facem.

IV. 13

At last the gods have listened to my prayers!
Yes, Lycia, you have become a crone.
You still think, Lycia, that with another drink
You can rouse yourself, and still stir Cupid too.

But, though you woo him in your quavering voice,
Cupid's entranced by Chia, fair and nubile,
Whose harp has touched him with her song.
He flies past withered oaks to admire young flowers,

He shrinks from yellow teeth and wrinkled skin.
Silk robes and precious gems once added to your grace.
Now they can't conceal your ugly face and clumsy gait.
Time stole you away who stole me from myself.

You were denied an early grave who once rejoiced
At the death of Cinara, your only rival.
You lived too long, outlived my early passion.
The book that recorded your charms is locked forever.

Cinara was given the gift of an early death
So the echo of her loveliness would linger.
Not for you, old crow, now teased by cruel young men
Who laugh at the burnt-out torch: your beauty's ashes.

Carolyn Kizer

Quae cura patrum quaeve Quiritium
plenis honorum muneribus tuas,
   Auguste, virtutes in aevum
     per titulos memoresque fastus

aeternet, o, qua sol habitabiles
inlustrat oras, maxime principum,
   quem legis expertes Latinae
     Vindelici didicere nuper,

quid Marte posses. milite nam tuo
Drusus Genaunos, implacidum genus,
   Breunosque veloces et arces
     Alpibus impositas tremendis

deiecit acer plus vice simplici;
maior Neronum mox grave proelium
   commisit immanesque Raetos
     auspiciis pepulit secundis,

spectandus in certamine Martio
devota morti pectora liberae
   quantis fatigaret ruinis,
     indomitas prope qualis undas

exercet Auster Pleiadum choro
scindente nubes, impiger hostium
   vexare turmas et frementem
     mittere equum medios per ignes.

sic tauriformis volvitur Aufidus,
qui regna Dauni praefluit Apuli,
   cum saevit horrendamque cultis
     diluviem minitatur agris,

IV. 14

By what means care the fathers and citizens
to fully honor and reward you,
    Augustus, for your splendor, forever
        through inscriptions and commemorations

immortalize you, O mightiest of princes, wherever
the sun shines on habitable places?
    Whose vigor in war the Vindelici,
        with no experience of Roman rule,

have just learned! For with your soldiers
fierce Drusus, doubling the revenge,
    cast down the remorseless Genauni,
        and swift Breuni, and their strongholds

perched high on the terrible Alps.
Soon too the elder Nero weighed into battle,
    and under favorable signs, crushed
        the savage Rhaetians,

a spectacular sight to witness in battle
as he smashed the hearts of those
    who would celebrate the deaths
        of free men, like the South Wind

splitting the wild waves, when dancing
Pleiades break through the clouds,
    keen to harass the ranks of the enemy,
        his snorting horse roaring through fire.

As bull-bodied Aufidus rolls on and on
past the realms of Apulian Daunus,
    grows savage and threatens prime farmland
        with a dreadful flood,

ut barbarorum Claudius agmina
ferrata vasto diruit impetu
   primosque et extremos metendo
      stravit humum sine clade victor,

te copias, te consilium et tuos
praebente divos. nam tibi quo die
   portus Alexandrea supplex
      et vacuam patefecit aulam,

Fortuna lustro prospera tertio
belli secundos reddidit exitus,
   laudemque et optatum peractis
      imperiis decus adrogavit.

te Cantaber non ante domabilis
Medusque et Indus, te profugus Scythes
   miratur, o tutela praesens
      Italiae dominaeque Romae.

te, fontium qui celat origines,
Nilusque et Hister, te rapidus Tigris,
   te beluosus qui remotis
      obstrepit Oceanus Britannis,

te non paventis funera Galliae
duraeque tellus audit Hiberiae
   te caede gaudentes Sygambri
      compositis venerantur armis.

so Claudius assaulted the ironclad hordes
of savages, leaving them strewn over the field
    as he mowed down vanguard and rear,
        a total victory, without loss—

the troops were yours, the plan was yours,
the gods offered by you. And, on the very day
    Alexandria bowed down and opened her
        harbor and empty palace to you,

good Fortune, three times five years later,
brought a happy end to the war,
    and brought praise and sought-after glory
        to those who enacted your commands.

The Cantabrian, never before conquered,
the Mede and the Indian, the wandering Scythian,
    all marvel at you, great protector
        of Italy and imperial Rome.

The Nile conceals the source of its springs
but hears you; so too the Hister, the rapid Tigris,
    and the Ocean infested with monsters
        that howls around remote Britain,

and Gaul, full of scorn for death, and the harsh
land of Iberia! The slaughter-loving Sygambri
    have laid down their weapons
        and venerate your name.

John Kinsella

Phoebus volentem proelia me loqui
victas et urbes increpuit lyra,
    ne parva Tyrrhenum per aequor
        vela darem. tua, Caesar, aetas

fruges et agris rettulit uberes
et signa nostro restituit Iovi
    derepta Parthorum superbis
        postibus et vacuum duellis

Ianum Quirini clausit et ordinem
rectum evaganti frena licentiae
    iniecit emovitque culpas
        et veteres revocavit artes,

per quas Latinum nomen et Italae
crevere vires famaque et imperi
    porrecta maiestas ad ortus
        solis ab Hesperio cubili.

custode rerum Caesare non furor
civilis aut vis exiget otium,
    non ira, quae procudit enses
        et miseras inimicat urbes.

non qui profundum Danuvium bibunt
edicta rumpent Iulia, non Getae,
    non Seres infidive Persae,
        non Tanain prope flumen orti.

nosque et profestis lucibus et sacris
inter iocosi munera Liberi
    cum prole matronisque nostris,
        rite deos prius adprecati,

virtute functos more patrum duces
Lydis remixto carmine tibiis
    Troiamque et Anchisen et almae
        progeniem Veneris canemus.

IV. 15

Apollo struck his lyre and forbad I sing
Of combat and conquered lands, or launch
   My little craft on stormy epic seas.
      Your rule, Augustus,

Has brought bounty to our fields, restored
To our gods those standards stripped from proud
   Parthian columns, closed the iron doors
      To the temple of war,

Reined in the recklessness of those who would swerve
From the straight course, banished wickedness,
   And called us back to those ancient ways
      By which the Latin name,

The power of Rome, the fame and majesty
Of her empire have been gloriously extended
   From where the bright sun first rises
      Even to its westernmost bed.

While Caesar stands guard, no turmoil at home,
No arms abroad can unbalance the peace,
   And no wrath that forges swords
      Shall beset our cities.

None shall break the Julian laws, not those
Who drink from the Danube, neither the Getes
   Nor the Seres, neither the faithless Persian
      Nor the fierce Scythian.

So whether it be an ordinary or a sacred day,
Amidst the blessings of beaming Bacchus,
   With our wives and children, let us
      First, as is fit, offer prayers,

Then to the lilt of Lydian pipes, let us sing
As our forefathers did, of the noble dead,
   Of the fall of Troy, of old Anchises,
      And the sons of gracious Venus.

J. D. McClatchy

NOTES ON THE TRANSLATORS

ROBERT BLY, who lives in Minneapolis, was born in Minnesota in 1926. He graduated from Harvard and received his M.A. in 1956 from the University of Iowa. Among his thirty books of poetry are *What Have I Ever Lost By Dying: Collected Prose Poems* (1992), *Morning Poems* (1997), *Eating the Honey of Words: New and Selected Poems* (1999), and *The Night Abraham Called to the Stars* (2001); *The Light Around the Body* (1967) won the National Book Award. He has translated the work of many poets, including Rumi, Kabir, Lorca, Neruda, Machado, Rilke, and Tranströmer.

EAVAN BOLAND was born in Dublin, Ireland, in 1944, and educated in London, New York, and Dublin. She is now a professor of English at Stanford, and earlier taught at Trinity College, University College, Iowa, and Bowdoin. Her most recent collection is *Against Love Poetry* (2001), and earlier books include *An Origin Like Water: Collected Poems 1967–1987* (1996). She is also the author of *Object Lessons: The Life of the Woman and the Poet in Our Times* (1995), and with Mark Strand has edited *The Making of a Poem* (2000).

ROBERT CREELEY was born in Arlington, Massachusetts, in 1926, and was educated at Harvard. In 1954 he began teaching at Black Mountain College, where he edited the *Black Mountain Review,* dedicated to experimental work. He has published books of fiction, prose, essays and interviews, and more than sixty collections of poetry, including *Selected Poems 1945–1990* (1991), *Life & Death* (1998), and *Just in Time: Poems 1984–1994* (2001). In 2001 he was given the Lannan Lifetime Achievement Award. Since 1989, he has taught at the State University of New York, Buffalo. He was elected a Chancellor of the Academy of American Poets in 1999.

DICK DAVIS was born in Portsmouth, England, in 1945, graduated from King's College, Cambridge, and later studied Persian, a subject he now teaches at Ohio State University. He has translated works by Natalia Ginzburg, as well as by many Persian writers, among them Attar's *The Conference of the Birds,* and *The Legend of Seyavash* from Ferdowsi's *Shahnamah*. His first book of poems, *In the Distance,* appeared in 1975, and his *Selected and New Poems* was published in 1991. His most recent collection is *Belonging* (2002).

MARK DOTY was born in Maryville, Tennessee, in 1953. His sixth book of poems, *Source,* appeared in 2001. An earlier collection, *My Alexandria,* was given the National Book Critics Circle Award in 1993, and in 1995, Britain's T. S. Eliot Prize. His memoir, *Heaven's Coast* (1996), won the PEN/Martha Albrand Award. A second memoir, *Firebird,* appeared in 1999, and *Still Life with Oysters and Lemons* in 2001. He teaches in the graduate program at the University of Houston, and divides his time between Houston and Provincetown.

ALICE FULTON has published five books of poetry: *Dance Script with Electric Ballerina* (1982), *Palladium* (1985), *Powers of Congress* (1990), *Sensual Math* (1995), and *Felt* (2001). A collection of prose, *Feeling as a Foreign Language: The Good Strangeness of Poetry,* appeared in 1999. She has received fellowships from the MacArthur and Guggenheim Foundations. For many years she taught at the University of Michigan, Ann Arbor; she now teaches at Cornell.

DEBORA GREGER was born in Colorado in 1949 and raised in Washington. She is a graduate of the University of Washington and of the writing program at Iowa. She has written six books of poems, including *The 1002nd Night* (1990), *Desert Fathers, Uranium Daughters* (1996), and *God* (2001). Among her honors are an Award in Literature from the American Academy of Arts and Letters, and the Brandeis University Award in Poetry. She teaches at the University of Florida, and divides her time between Florida and England.

LINDA GREGERSON is the author of three books of poetry, *Fire in the Conservatory* (1983), *The Woman Who Died in Her Sleep* (1996), and *Waterborne* (2002). In addition, she has written two books of prose, *The Reformation of the Subject: Spenser, Milton, and the English Protestant Epic* (1995) and *Negative Capability: Contemporary American Poetry* (2001). She teaches at the University of Michigan, Ann Arbor.

RACHEL HADAS, whose father, Moses Hadas, was a distinguished classicist, was born in New York City in 1948. Her most recent collection of poems is *Indelible* (2001); among her many other collections is *Halfway Down the Hall: New and Selected Poems* (1998). A book of her translations, *Other Worlds Than This,* was published in 1994, and includes works by Euripides, Tibullus, Rimbaud, and Baudelaire. In addition, she has translated Seneca's *Oedipus.* Her critical books include *Form, Cycle, Infinity: Landscape Imagery in the Poetry of Robert Frost and George Seferis* (1985), and *Merrill, Cavafy, Poems, and Dreams* (2000). She teaches English at Rutgers University, Newark.

306

DONALD HALL was born in New Haven, Connecticut, in 1928 and is a graduate of Harvard and Oxford. Among his many collections of poems are *The One Day* (1988), which won the National Book Critics Circle Award, and *The Happy Man* (1986), which won the Lenore Marshall Poetry Prize. His most recent collection is *The Painted Bed* (2002). In addition, he has written memoirs, books for children, essays, plays, and stories, and has edited more than two dozen textbooks and anthologies.

ROBERT HASS, who served as U.S. Poet Laureate from 1995 to 1997, was born in San Francisco in 1941. His first book of poems, *Field Guide,* was published in 1973 as part of the Yale Younger Poets series. His subsequent books are *Praise* (1979), *Human Wishes* (1989), and *Sun Under Wood* (1996). A collection of his essays, *Twentieth Century Pleasures* (1984), won the National Book Critics Circle Award. He is a frequent translator of work by Czeslaw Milosz, and teaches at the University of California, Berkeley.

ANTHONY HECHT was born in New York City in 1923 and studied at Bard, Kenyon, and Columbia. He served overseas in the army during World War II and later pursued a teaching career at Bard, Smith, the University of Rochester, and Georgetown. He was awarded the Pulitzer Prize in 1968 for *The Hard Hours,* and the Bollingen Prize in 1983. From 1982 until 1984 he served as consultant in poetry to the Library of Congress. His latest collection of poems is *The Darkness and the Light* (2001). With Helen Bacon he translated Aeschylus's *Seven Against Thebes,* and he has written four books of criticism, most recently *Melodies Unheard* (2002).

DARYL HINE was born in British Columbia in 1936, left Canada in 1962, and has since lived in Europe and in the United States, where for many years he was editor of *Poetry* magazine. His *Selected Poems* was published in 1980; among his other collections of poetry are *In and Out* (1989) and *Postscripts* (1991). He has published a novel and a travel book, along with a series of notable translations from the Greek and Latin classics, including Theocritus, Ovid, and the Homeric Hymns, and most recently *Puerilities* (2001), a selection of erotic epigrams from *The Greek Anthology.*

JOHN HOLLANDER, recently retired from Yale where he taught for many years, is a remarkably versatile man of letters. He was born in New York City in 1929. His first book of poems appeared in 1958, chosen by W. H. Auden for the Yale Younger Poets series; later collections include *Selected Poetry* (1993) and *Figurehead* (1999). A distinguished scholar of Renaissance literature, he is also an inventive critic whose many books of commentary include *The Gazer's Spirit* (1995) and *The Work of Poetry* (1997). He has also written libretti, books for children, an influential guide to English verse, and many translations. He was awarded the Bollingen Prize in 1983.

RICHARD HOWARD was born in Cleveland, Ohio, in 1929, and educated at Columbia and the Sorbonne. After working for several years as a lexicographer, he became a translator from the French and has published over 150 titles, including work by Stendhal, Roland Barthes, André Gide, and E. M. Cioran. In 1983 he received the American Book Award for his translation of Baudelaire's *Fleurs du mal*. In 1970 he won the Pulitzer Prize for his own poetry, volumes of which include *Like Most Revelations* (1994) and *Trappings* (1999). In addition, he has published two critical studies, serves as poetry editor of *The Paris Review,* and teaches in the writing division of Columbia.

JOHN KINSELLA was born in 1963 in Perth, Western Australia. He has published more than a dozen books of his poems in Australia, several of which have appeared as well in Britain, including *Poems 1980–1994* (1998) and *The Hunt* (1998). A book of prose fiction, *Genre,* was published in 1997. He teaches at Kenyon College and is a Fellow of Churchill College, Cambridge. He divides his time between England, Australia, and the United States. His selected poems and selected essays are forthcoming.

CAROLYN KIZER was born in 1925 in Spokane, Washington, graduated from Sarah Lawrence, and studied further at Columbia and the University of Washington. From 1966 until 1970 she was the first director of literary programs at the National Endowment for the Arts. Her first book of poems, *The Ungrateful Garden,* appeared in 1961; her fifth, *Yin,* was awarded the 1985 Pulitzer Prize; her most recent is *Cool, Calm & Collected: Poems 1960–2000* (2000). *Proses* (1994) is a collection of her essays. She has also translated from many languages.

JAMES LASDUN was born in London in 1958 and studied at Bristol University. He now lives in New York. His first book of stories, *Delirium Eclipse* (1985), was followed by *Three Evenings* (1992). He is the author of three collections of poetry, *A Jump Start* (1987), *Woman Police Officer in Elevator* (1997), and *Landscape with Chainsaw* (2001). With Michael Hofmann, he edited *After Ovid: New Metamorphoses* (1995).

J. D. McCLATCHY was born in Bryn Mawr, Pennsylvania, in 1945, and was educated at Georgetown and Yale. He is the author of five collections of poetry, including *Ten Commandments* (1999) and *Hazmat* (2002). He has also written two books of literary essays, most recently *Twenty Questions* (1999), and several opera libretti. He is editor of *The Voice of the Poet* series, and has edited many other books, including a revised edition of *The Vintage Book of Contemporary American Poetry*. He teaches at Yale, and edits *The Yale Review.*

HEATHER McHUGH was born to Canadian parents in San Diego, California, in 1948. She was raised in Virginia, educated at Harvard, and is now the Milliman Distinguished Writer-in-Residence at the University of Washington. Among her collections are *Hinge & Sign: Poems 1968–1993* (1994) and *The Father of Predicaments*

(1999). A book of essays, *Broken English: Poetry and Partiality,* appeared in 1993. She has translated Euripides' *Cyclops,* and the poetry of Jean Follain. With Nikolai Popov, she has collaborated on translations of Blaga Dimitrova and Paul Celan. In 1999 she was named a Chancellor of the Academy of American Poets.

W. S. MERWIN was born in New York City in 1927, the son of a minister. After graduating from Princeton, he lived abroad, working as a tutor (first to the children of Robert Graves) and a translator. He has lived for long periods in England and France, and now lives in Hawaii. He has published twenty-two books of translations, their authors ranging from Persius and Dante to Mandelstam and Neruda. His seventeen collections of poems include *The Folding Cliffs: A Narrative* (1998) and *The Pupil* (2001). He has been awarded the Pulitzer Prize, the Bollingen Prize, and the Tanning Prize for mastery in the art of poetry.

PAUL MULDOON was born in Portadown, County Armagh, Northern Ireland, in 1951, and studied at Queen's University, Belfast. He worked for many years in Belfast as a BBC producer, but since 1987 has lived in the United States and now teaches at Princeton. His *Poems 1968–1998* (2001) gathers work from eight previous volumes. In 1994 he won the T. S. Eliot Prize. He has also published translations—notably of Aristophanes' *The Birds*, with Richard Martin—and opera libretti. In 1999, he was elected Professor of Poetry at Oxford.

CARL PHILLIPS, born in 1959, was educated at Harvard—where he did his undergraduate work in Classics—and at Boston University, where he studied creative writing after eight years as a high school Latin teacher. His first book of poems, *In the Blood,* appeared in 1992. Five others have followed: *Cortège* (1995), *From the Devotions* (1998), *Pastoral* (2000), *The Tether* (2001), and *Rock Harbor* (2002); his translation of Sophocles' *Philoctetes* is forthcoming. The recipient of the 2002 Kingsley Tufts Prize, he is a Professor of English at Washington University in St. Louis.

ROBERT PINSKY was born in 1940, raised in Long Branch, New Jersey, and educated at Rutgers and Stanford. Among his six collections of poems are *The Figured Wheel: New and Collected Poems 1966–1996* (1996) and *Jersey Rain* (2000). He is the author of several books of criticism, and of an acclaimed translation of Dante's *Inferno* (1994). In 1997 he was appointed Poet Laureate of the United States, a position he held for three years. Creator and director of the Favorite Poem Project and poetry editor of *Slate,* he teaches in the graduate writing program at Boston University.

MARIE PONSOT, born in New York City in 1921, published her first book, *True Minds,* in 1957 as part of the City Lights Pocket Poets series. It was followed by *Admit Impediment* (1981), *The Green Dark* (1988), *The Bird Catcher* (1998), and

Springing: New and Selected Poems (2002). She has translated dozens of books, many of them books for children, from the French. Her *Love and Folly: Selected Fables and Tales of La Fontaine* also appeared in 2002.

CHARLES SIMIC was born in Yugoslavia in 1938, and emigrated with his family to the United States in 1954. His memories of those early years are recounted in his memoir, *A Fly in the Soup* (2000). Among his many books of poems are *Selected Early Poems* (1999), *Night Picnic* (2001), and *The World Doesn't End: Prose Poems,* which received the Pulitzer Prize in 1990. He has worked tirelessly as a translator from the Serbian, and his *The Horse Has Six Legs: An Anthology of Serbian Poetry* appeared in 1992. Since 1973, he has taught English at the University of New Hampshire.

MARK STRAND was born in 1934 on Prince Edward Island in Canada but raised in the United States, where he graduated from Antioch College and then attended both the Yale Art School and the Iowa Writers Workshop. His first book of poems appeared in 1964, and his most recent, *Blizzard of One,* was awarded the 1999 Pulitzer Prize. He has published two books of translations—one, with Thomas Colchie, of poems by the Brazilian Carlos Drummond de Andrade, the other, of poems by the Spaniard Rafael Alberti. In addition he has written several collections of prose and three books about art. In 1990 he was named the nation's fourth Poet Laureate.

CHARLES TOMLINSON was born in 1927 in Stoke-on-Trent in England and went to Queens' College, Cambridge. At the start of his career he was better known in America, and the influence of such American poets as Wallace Stevens and William Carlos Williams has been decisive. His *Collected Poems* was published in 1980. A collection of his translations appeared in 1983, and included work by Ungaretti, Paz, Machado, and Tyutchev. He also edited the *Oxford Book of Verse in English Translation* (1980). He began teaching at the University of Bristol in 1957.

ELLEN BRYANT VOIGT was born in 1943 in Danville, Virginia. She has published six volumes of poetry: *Claiming Kin* (1976), *The Forces of Plenty* (1983), *The Lotus Flowers* (1987), *Two Trees* (1992), *Kyrie* (1995), and *Shadow of Heaven* (2002). Her essays on poetry are collected in *The Flexible Lyric* (1999). She has long taught in the Warren Wilson College M.F.A. Program, and she is currently the Vermont State Poet.

DAVID WAGONER was born in 1926 in Ohio, and studied under Theodore Roethke at Pennsylvania State University. Since 1954 he has lived in Seattle; he recently retired from the University of Washington, where for many years he has also edited *Poetry Northwest.* His first book of poems, *Dry Sun, Dry Wind,* appeared in 1953. *Traveling Light: Collected and New Poems* was published in 1999. He has also written ten novels, and is a Chancellor Emeritus of the Academy of American Poets.

310

ROSANNA WARREN was born in Fairfield, Connecticut, in 1953, and educated at Yale. She has published three collections of poems, *Snow Day* (1981), *Each Leaf Shines Separate* (1984), and *Stained Glass* (1993), which received the Lamont Prize from the Academy of American Poets. She has also won prizes from the American Academy of Arts and Letters and the Lila Wallace Foundation. She has, with Stephen Scully, published a translation of Euripides' *Suppliant Women,* and in 1989 edited *The Art of Translation: Voices from the Field.* In 1999 she was named a Chancellor of the Academy of American Poets.

RICHARD WILBUR, born in 1921, published his first book of poems, *The Beautiful Changes,* in 1947, and his most recent, *Mayflies,* in 2000. In 1989, while he was serving as Poet Laureate, his *New and Collected Poems* appeared, and won for him a second Pulitzer Prize. He has translated from several languages, but his versions of Molière and Racine are especially prized. His most recently translated play is Molière's *The Bungler.* He has also published two collections of essays, *Responses* (1976) and *The Catbird's Song* (1997). He lives in Cummington, Massachusetts, and in Key West.

C. K. WILLIAMS was born in Newark, New Jersey, in 1936, and studied at Bucknell and the University of Pennsylvania. His first book of poems, *Lies,* appeared in 1969. His fifth book, *Flesh and Blood,* won the 1987 National Book Critics Circle Award, and his most recent book, *Repair,* won the Pulitzer Prize in 2000. His two books of prose are *Poetry and Consciousness* (1998) and *Misgivings* (2000). He has also published translations of Sophocles' *Women of Trachis,* Euripides' *The Bacchae,* and the poems of Issa. He divides his time between Princeton and Paris.

CHARLES WRIGHT was born in Pickwick Dam, Tennessee, in 1935. During army service in Italy, he discovered the work of Ezra Pound and dedicated himself to a career in poetry. He is now poet-in-residence at the University of Virginia, and for his work has received the National Book Award and the Pulitzer Prize. His major work is collected in three trilogies, *Country Music* (1982), *The World of the Ten Thousand Things* (1990), and *Negative Blue* (2000). He has published two books of essays and two books of translations from the Italian of Eugenio Montale and Dino Campana.

STEPHEN YENSER, born in Wichita, Kansas, in 1941, is the author of a book of poems, *The Fire in All Things,* which won the Walt Whitman Award from the Academy of American Poets. He has also written several books of criticism, among them *Circle to Circle: The Poetry of Robert Lowell* (1975), *The Consuming Myth: The Work of James Merrill* (1987), and *A Boundless Field: American Poetry at Large* (2002), and is the co-editor of James Merrill's *Collected Poems* (2001) and *Collected Novels and Plays* (2002). He is professor of English and director of creative writing at the University of California, Los Angeles.